MAKING INDIA AWESOME

Chetan Bhagat is the author of seven blockbuster books. These include six novels—*Five Point Someone* (2004), *One Night @ the Call Center* (2005), *The 3 Mistakes of My Life* (2008), *2 States* (2009), *Revolution 2020* (2011), *Half Girlfriend* (2014)—and the non-fiction title *What Young India Wants* (2012).

Chetan's books have remained bestsellers since their release. Many of his novels have been adapted into successful Bollywood films.

The *New York Times* called him 'the biggest-selling English language novelist in India's history'. *TIME* magazine named him amongst the '100 most influential people in the world' and Fast Company, USA, listed him as one of the world's '100 most creative people in business'.

Chetan writes columns for leading English and Hindi newspapers, focusing on youth and national development issues. He is also a motivational speaker and screenplay writer.

Chetan quit his international investment banking career in 2009 to devote his entire time to writing and make change happen in the country. He lives in Mumbai with his wife, Anusha, an ex-classmate from IIM-A, and his twin boys, Shyam and Ishaan.

CHETAN BHAGAT

MAKING INDIA AWESOME

New Essays & Columns

RUPA

Published by
Rupa Publications India Pvt. Ltd 2015
7/16, Ansari Road, Daryaganj
New Delhi 110002

Sales centres:
Allahabad Bengaluru Chennai
Hyderabad Jaipur Kathmandu
Kolkata Mumbai

ISBN: 978-81-291-3742-5

First impression 2015

10 9 8 7 6 5 4 3 2 1

The moral right of the author has been asserted.

Printed at Manipal Technologies Ltd, Manipal

To the awesome youth of India

Contents

Making India Awesome: A Letter to the Reader   1

AWESOME GOVERNANCE: POLITICS AND ECONOMY

POLITICS

Seventeen Commandments for Narendra Modi   19
Games Politicians Play   23
Revenge of the Oppressed: Why Corruption
Continues to Be Around Despite the Outcry Against It   25
We the Shameless   28
The Kings in Our Minds   31
The Telangana Effect   34
Analysing the Modi Effect   37
Can India's Backward Polity Provide a Pro-growth
Economic Environment?   40
Rahul's New Clothes, and the Naked Truth   44
Swachh Congress Abhiyan: Some Essential Steps   48
Once upon a Beehive   55

ECONOMY

Rescue the Nation   59
To Make 'Make in India' Happen, Delete Control   62
Pro-poor or Pro-poverty?   65
The Tiny-bang Theory for Setting Off Big-bang Reforms   68

AWESOME SOCIETY: WHO WE ARE AS A PEOPLE AND WHAT WE NEED TO CHANGE

Time to Face Our Demons	75
We Have Let Them Down	79
Watching the Nautch Girls	82
Let's Talk about Sex	85
The Real Dirty Picture	89
Saying Cheers in Gujarat	92
Our Fatal Attraction to Food	96
Cleanliness Begins at Home	99
India-stupid and India-smart	102
Bhasha Bachao, Roman Hindi Apnao	105
Mangalyaan+Unlucky Tuesdays	108
A Ray of Hope	111
Junk Food's Siren Appeal	114

AWESOME EQUALITY: WOMEN'S RIGHTS, GAY RIGHTS AND MINORITY RIGHTS

WOMEN'S RIGHTS

Ladies, Stop Being so Hard on Yourself	121
Five Things Women Need to Change about Themselves	124
Home Truths on Career Wives	127
Wake up and Respect Your Inner Queen	130
Indian Men Should Channelize Their Inner Mr Mary Kom	133
Fifty Shades of Fair: Why Colour Gets under Our Skin	136

GAY RIGHTS

Section 377 Is Our Collective Sin	139

MINORITY RIGHTS

Letter from an Indian Muslim Youth	143

Being Hindu Indian or Muslim Indian   146
It's Not Moderate Muslims' Fault   150
Mapping the Route to Minority Success   154

AWESOME RESOURCES: THE YOUTH
An Open Letter to Indian Change Seekers   159
We, the Half-educated People   162
DU-ing It All Wrong, Getting It All Mixed Up   166
How the Youth Can Get Their Due   169
Scored Low in Exams? Some Life Lessons from a
76-Percenter   172

Concluding Thoughts   175

Before you begin reading, it might be helpful to understand the words that comprise the title, so that we know the task at hand better.

Making /ˈmeɪkɪŋ/ *verb*
1. to bring into existence, to produce; bring about; render.
2. to convert from one state, condition, category, etc., to another.

India /ˈɪndɪə/ *noun*
Officially the Republic of India; a country in South Asia. It is the seventh-largest country by area, the second-most populous country with over 1.2 billion people, and the most populous democracy in the world.

Awesome /ˈɔːs(ə)m/ *adjective*
1. causing or inducing awe; inspiring an overwhelming feeling of reverence, admiration, or fear: an awesome sight.
2. exhibiting or marked by awe; showing reverence, admiration, or fear.
3. *informal.* very impressive: typically used by the Internet generation.

Making India Awesome:
A Letter to the Reader

Dear Reader,

Thank you for picking up this book. This is not a story. There is no romance in here, nor are there page-turning, thrilling moments. Rather, this book is about a dream both you and I share—to make India a better place.

Why This Book?

The current political environment and public sentiment are so cynical that one wonders if there is even a point in writing a book about a better India.

As I sit down to write this opening essay, I hear political noise everywhere. The ruling party, the Bharatiya Janata Party (BJP), brought to power a year ago with love and votes, is now in the midst of battling several controversies. Cabinet ministers are accused of helping a fugitive; the fugitive, on his part, is trying to lay blame on multiple senior politicians. State government scams are coming to the fore in Maharashtra and Madhya Pradesh, one of them triggering many deaths. The bane of favouritism is back—with the news that a flight full of passengers was held up for an hour because an Indian Administrative Service (IAS) officer in a chief minister's contingent forgot his correct passport at home. The prime minister hasn't spoken about any of these issues, even while everyone else is talking about them. The Congress is blaming the BJP. The BJP is reminding the

Congress about its past sins. Their followers on Twitter are sending abusive tweets to one another.

The image I have presented is a snapshot of Indian news right now, but this could be the situation at any given point in time. There is nothing unusual about such noise. Chances are that if you happen to read this some years later, and turn on the television, you will see a couple of fresh, new controversies—with a lot of debating, pontificating, finger-pointing, outrage and no problem-solving. The noise from one controversy will ultimately fade and make way for the next…and then, the next.

Youth and National Consciousness

With all this chaos, an average viewer or reader will either be totally confused, or, more likely, will opt out of the constant cacophony generated by unsolvable national issues. No surprise then that most of India's youth don't care much about politics or the government.

Applying the 80:20 rule, I would say that 80 per cent of our youth don't even care about politics or government. What they care about are their lives—*their* jobs, *their* boyfriends or girlfriends and, well, that's about it. We can call this set of people *Self-focused Indifferent Indians*. This is a huge segment, and the actual number of people who just don't care about what happens may be even higher than 80 per cent!

Of the remaining 20 per cent who do care, most have decided to take permanent sides, as this helps solve confusion. These sides are often based on a personality. For example, it's just simpler to assume that Modi is always right, or that Kejriwal is the person to back, no matter what. The derogatory terms, 'Modi-bhakt' and 'AAPtard', have emerged because of this set of people. They are politically conscious, but are aligned. They defend anything their chosen party says, and are ready to abuse and insult anyone who even hints at disagreeing with their great leader. Such people create a lot of noise on social media and may be well-intentioned about the country; however, they solve nothing. They have taken sides and stick to them, no matter what the issue. Hence, their contribution to public discourse is limited. Again, using the 80:20 rule, 80 per cent of people who care about politics and national issues fall in the 'taking sides' category. We can call these people *Caring but Aligned Indians.*

Finally, there is the tiny segment that matters—people who actually care about the country, have an interest in political issues, but don't have fixed sides. These are—to do the maths—20 per cent of the 20 per cent, or a mere *4 per cent* of our youth. We can call this narrow set of people—*Caring Objective Indians.* These are the people who give me hope. For they want to give support to the right issue, not to a particular party. And if we have enough people of this kind, we can actually put India on the right path.

This book is an attempt to reach out to, and expand the narrow segment of, Caring Objective Indians.

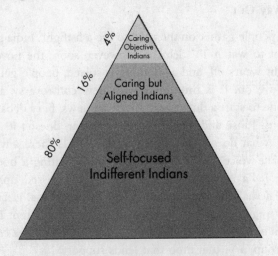

The Sad State of Caring Objective Indians

Caring Objective Indians are often ignored or shouted down in debates. They are also labelled as fence-sitters, opportunists, or indecisive, confused, contradictory or weak.

Say, a Caring Objective Indian, who wanted change, voted for the BJP in the Lok Sabha elections. However, the same voter dislikes the way the BJP is handling the current controversies. When he voices his protest, Caring but Aligned Indians will attack him. BJP supporters will call him ignorant and label him an idiot. Non-BJP supporters will abuse him and question why the hell did he vote for the BJP. Faced with such attack, the Caring Objective Indian will withdraw and eventually become silent. Every issue will, therefore, become a free-for-all between the already aligned sets, each side shouting down the other. Such screaming and blaming solves nothing, though the emotions and whipped-up drama entertain for a while and make for good TV. After all, it is fun to see educated people shout and belittle other educated people!

The Way Out

Just as people gather on the road to see a fistfight, India gathers at night to watch TV debates. However, soon, the novelty of the fight wears off, and as nothing is solved, people get bored and move on. It is time then for a new controversy, and for each side to start a duel again. Breaking news, fiery debates, no solutions. Rinse and repeat. Sounds familiar, doesn't it?

So, what do we do in such a scenario? Is there any room for a sane voice? Is there even a point to writing a book like *Making India Awesome* when things are so messed up? Does anyone actually want solutions instead of the drama? Is it simply easier to ignore it all, and be a Self-focused Indifferent Indian? Or even better, to become aligned and at least have the comfort of a group, a virtual mob that lends support?

All these doubts bubbled up in my head when I conceived this book. Ultimately, I felt there is a need for this. In all the noise, there are people who would care for a voice to simplify things and point to a solution. Thus, this book was born. The fact that you have picked it up means that, at least to a certain extent, I was right; there are Caring Objective Indians who want to hear reason.

India 2015 versus India 2011–2014

I think it is interesting to compare the mood of the nation now versus a couple of years ago. In 2012, when my book *What Young India Wants* was published, not only was I a different person, but I was also looking at a different India. How so? Did this nation not have problems then?

Sure, we did. We had tons of issues then, and some would argue we had them on a much larger scale. The mind-boggling numbers associated with the CWG, 2G and coal scams prove this. These cases shocked some of the most indifferent Indians, and brought to the fore a problem each one of us faces—corruption. The growth of social media, which allowed accumulation and aggregation of public opinion like never before, helped coalesce people's anger against corruption.

The United Progressive Alliance (UPA) government in power then—a Congress-led hotchpotch coalition—missed all this until it was too late. Neither did the government act quickly on the scams, nor did it sense public anger fast enough. Meanwhile, we had street protests, hunger strikes, social media hashtags and a sort of a mini-Arab Spring, all in the span of two years.

In all this frustration, something was different from what we have today. In 2012, we felt anger instead of cynicism. We also knew how to give our fury direction—we believed that the Congress-led government was at fault. This party—ruling the country for sixty-odd years and in power for 90 per cent of Independent India's life—seemed to be the obvious reason for the nation's woes.

2011–2014 Recap: The Anna Movement, AAP and Modi

The massive anti-government sentiment of 2011 was amplified by the media and solidified by new social media. It led to the rise of several phenomena. One of these was the Anna Hazare movement, an anti-corruption drive that sought to have a Lokpal, or an independent ombudsman, in the country. The fact that the movement had an end game, a solution of sorts, made it different from previous protests against corruption. People from all walks of life backed it, including me. Had the government relented with a reasonable Lokpal, the movement might have taken a natural course. However, the UPA government dithered and the Anna movement created a new political party, the Aam Aadmi Party (AAP). While Anna Hazare withdrew from the political entity, it gave birth to a new political star called Arvind Kejriwal. Smart, well-intentioned, media-savvy, relatively young and from a humble background, Kejriwal was ready to take on anyone in the establishment. His passion and aggression won him many fans, and even though we didn't have a Lokpal, people saw Kejriwal as one of the solutions to India's crises. While Kejriwal's journey to power in Delhi is well known, it is only now that his position has assumed some stability as the state chief minister.

Before his recent electoral victory (in February 2015), Kejriwal was inconsistent, exhibiting traits that showed earnestness but also inexperience. While people liked him, wanted him to have a future in Indian politics and knew that he could take on the Congress, they weren't sure that he could be a viable alternative to it.

Hence, this created another gap and simultaneously led to

the rise of another political star—Narendra Modi. The current prime minister of India was then the four-time chief minister of Gujarat, one of India's most affluent states. He belonged to the BJP, the Congress's traditional rival, and thus offered an alternative to the Congress. Unlike Kejriwal, Modi had far more political experience and a proven track record in running a state. In fact, his initiatives in promoting the successful Gujarat growth story cemented his position as an able administrator and visionary. While the Congress lost touch with the masses, Modi and the BJP began to echo popular sentiment—'Congress-Mukt Bharat', the war cry of the BJP, became instantly popular. Since Indians seem to like personalities in politics, the entire campaign revolved around Narendra Modi. 'Ab ki baar, Modi sarkar' was splattered across hoardings and newspapers in every city. The rest, as they say, is history.

The BJP won 282 seats, comfortably above the majority 271-mark in the Parliament. With its allies, the tally was well over 300. India was set to enter a new era. Publications around the world celebrated India's mandate for stability, and for a leader focused on development and not much else.

The Hindutva card of the BJP, something it had capitalized on in earlier elections, was kept aside; instead, the party promised an India that was committed to communal harmony as well as development. With great pomp and show, Modi was sworn in at the Rashtrapati Bhavan lawns. Thousands were present, including the heads of state of eight of our neighbouring countries.

Could it get any better for India?

2014 until Today: A Reality Check

The new government came to power. Things started to move. We had news reports of government employees being pulled up for not being punctual. Ministers worked long hours. Many pending government proposals began to get cleared. The prime minister announced initiatives like 'Swachh Bharat' or 'Clean India', which were well received.

And yet, not all expectations were met. The pace of economic reform, expected to accelerate with the new government, didn't change much. Many in the government managed expectations by saying, 'Don't expect big-bang reforms.' While the government launched a 'Make in India' campaign to invite foreign investors, reports of 'tax terrorism' multiplied, with overzealous tax departments hounding foreign institutional investors.

The education sector didn't transform significantly. Employment rate, often a result of economic growth, didn't pick up very much either. Communal statements from a few BJP leaders continued. The prime minister—vocal like no other prime ministerial candidate before the election—became more discreet. He spoke, but often about his own agenda, rather than about controversial or tricky issues.

The 'Modi wave', a sort of a fandom for Narendra Modi that had swept the nation before the election, turned into 'it's still early days, let's see what happens'.

The Ebbing Modi Wave

A strong sign that the Modi wave had ended came with the Delhi state elections of 2015. In February 2015, Arvind Kejriwal, won 67 out of the 70 seats in the Delhi Assembly. Several reasons were attributed to this landslide victory, including the fact that people wanted to give a real second chance to Arvind Kejriwal. However, one could not deny that the euphoria surrounding the new BJP government had ended, at least in Delhi.

Of course, soon after Kejriwal assumed power, controversies broke out about his government as well. The first came when Prashant Bhushan and Yogendra Yadav, two founding members of the AAP, were ousted from the party. Kejriwal was the only brand that mattered for the AAP; everyone else was dispensable. Another controversy involved the AAP law minister for Delhi forging his educational degrees. Then came the report about the AAP spending a mindboggling ₹500 crore plus for advertisements highlighting its own achievements.

Neither Modi nor Kejriwal seemed to have sustained their pre-election hype.

The Hope and Disappointment Cycle

So what's the pattern here? It seems that we, as Indians, do realize that there are problems in the system. However, to solve these problems, we place our faith in one messiah and bring him or her to power. Once we bring the messiah to power, we discover that s/he underwhelms us, getting trapped in controversies or hemmed in by limitations. From the Congress to the BJP to the AAP, every party seems to have tried its luck at the top in some capacity. However, no clear path is visible and the cycle of hope and disappointment continues. Change is slow, despite all of us agreeing that it is needed. We hear reports of how India is the next superpower about to take off. However, that take-off seems to have been stuck on the runway for a couple of decades now.

The realization that India's problems won't go away by changing a government creates both despair and hope.

First comes despair. It is disheartening to learn that we still haven't done enough to put India on the right path. After all, we did manage to have a Congress-mukt central government, the so-called cure. We also placed our two big political stars—Narendra Modi and Arvind Kejriwal—as prime minister and chief minister respectively, with a full majority. Yet the problems haven't ended. The faces have changed, not the issues.

Reality Check: The Despair

We are still far from being a confident superpower of the future. We are still a third world country with third world infrastructure; the roads in Mumbai still have potholes after the first rain! We do have a few achievements on the world stage in sports, science, defence or in spaces that ask for creativity. But we have millions of poor people. Job opportunities for the youth are limited. Economic growth is modest. Primary education is in poor shape. Most don't have access to quality healthcare.

I don't want to paint a sorry picture. However, before we get lost in our superpower-India fantasies and other such patriotic porn, it is important to face reality. Economic backwardness is not India's only bane. While a country like the USA has legalized gay marriage, we consider homosexuality illegal and are yet to repeal the draconian Section 377. Our women aren't treated well, and a whole bunch of gender issues such as female foeticide, sexual crimes against women, female malnutrition and discrimination against women at work exist in our society. Our religious minorities feel unsafe, and local Hindu–Muslim issues easily spiral into national unrest. All this is reason enough to believe that we are far from being awesome.

Awesome

Awesome is what I want to turn India into. Awesome is a term the young use to describe anything that is cool, aspirational, worthy of respect and that essentially inspires awe. While we all love our country, and that will never stop, to take it to awesome status needs some work.

Reality Check: The Hope

While the bitter truths about our system may create some gloom, there is also hope in present-day India. For unlike the

2011–2014 period, Indians today have a better grip on reality. For once, we don't think that there are a few bad guys at the top making all the mess. Fewer among us think that a messiah will come to save us. We finally have the niggling feeling that perhaps there's something wrong with *us*—that no law or leader can fix society unless society wants to fix itself. The realization that we are responsible for the mess we are in—and that it isn't 'their' fault—is the best hope India has had in decades.

Hence, our mild disillusionment with our political stars may not be a bad thing. They are not saviours, and it is unfair to expect them to be. It's not them, but *we*, who have to solve our problems.

How to Make a Nation Awesome

The anger and outrage on display between 2011 and 2014 wasn't wrong. In fact, we needed such fury to bring people together and acknowledge the problems we confronted. We may not have solved issues, but at least we tried to do something about them by protesting on the streets and voting for change. However, this wasn't enough, and now we know it.

Making a nation awesome takes more than just Twitter outrage, street protests and a toppling of governments in elections. It asks for a fundamental shift in societal values, culture and habits.

Transforming society's values is especially important. Let's take an example. If we want to eradicate the menace of corruption, every dishonest act must create deep revulsion within us. Fighting corruption is not restricted to naming and shaming a few corrupt officials. If we think it is okay to cheat in exams, lie to a ticket collector in the train about our kids' ages and pay a bit of money to avoid a big traffic fine, then at some level we clearly don't care about eliminating corruption all that much. At best, we hate the politician who gets to steal (while we don't!).

To take another example, it is unthinkable for Hindus to enter temples with their shoes on. Even so, why don't we, as Indians, cheat and enter places of worship covertly in our shoes? Simply because we feel it is disrespectful to do so. No law is needed; no politician at the top needs to remind us. It is our society's core values that guide us—we have learnt that places of worship should be treated with respect, and removing our shoes is one way of showing deference.

Now, if only we felt the same way about corruption! Well, hopefully we will, one day.

The Homogeneity Challenge

Spurring reform in a nation also requires homogeneity in thought. People should generally agree on what a country's top problems are and the solutions needed for them.

This is a massive challenge in India, one of the most diverse countries in the world. We have people from different cultures, communities, religions, ethnicities, income groups and educational backgrounds. Many get exasperated with India because we, its citizens, just never seem to get along. Some experts even say the idea of India is wrong; it is not more than a leftover patchwork of disparate kingdoms created by the British. After all, what does Kerala have in common with Assam, and what do the two share with Rajasthan? How can all these diverse groups ever agree?

There is some truth to such scepticism. Countries that have dramatically progressed in the last few decades—Taiwan, South Korea, Singapore and Japan—have a more homogenous population. Even China, a huge country, is culturally a lot less disparate than India.

Are we, as Indians, then fated to disagree with one another? Will our dreams be destroyed by internal disharmony? How will we ever become truly awesome?

My Role

This is where I feel I, and others like me, have a role. By God's grace and thanks to my readers' love, my books have reached almost all corners of the country.

Each book is a unique Indian story, about people from a particular place in India. The stories have worked all over India. Doesn't this mean that, at some level, we are homogenous? We can and do empathize with Krish Malhotra's attempts at getting married to a girl outside his community (*2 States*). A reader in Rajasthan can relate to Madhav Jha's struggle with spoken English (*Half Girlfriend*).

As a motivational speaker, I have travelled across India; I have visited over a hundred cities in the last three years. While there are geographical differences, I find that ultimately, as Indians, we are the same.

The average Indian anywhere in the country is looking for a better quality of life, a certain amount of hope and security and the freedom to make personal choices. The issues that really matter to us are the same. Differences exist, but they don't run as deep as our politicians would have us believe. A Maharashtrian father wants a good college for his son and doesn't care whether his MP is a Maharashtrian. An Assamese girl wants the freedom to marry her boyfriend, as does a woman in Karnataka.

This similarity of aspirations, at a fundamental level, is what gives me hope. It offers me—and others like me on a national platform—an opportunity to connect everyone. While fiction is fun and entertaining, writers like me also need to share common concerns with the population and propose a few deliverables.

Making India Awesome

It is my belief and conviction that if we all come together, we really can make our India awesome. We can have a nation that we are proud to be a part of and others choose to emulate.

We will do this by working on ourselves. The fix is not quick, and it won't come from electing an awesome messiah at the top. It will come from working on several aspects of our country.

For the sake of simplicity, I'll divide the work demanded of us to make India awesome into four main areas. These are:

- **Awesome Governance**: Making our government, politics and policies right
- **Awesome Society**: Fixing societal values, culture and habits
- **Awesome Equality**: Enforcing and respecting minority, gay and women's rights
- **Awesome Resources**: Utilizing our best resource pool—the youth

This has been graphically represented in the chart on the next page.

My columns over the past six years have tried to address each of these four areas; they have emphasized that our nation will become awesome only when we get an awesome report card in each of these four subjects.

All the noise and fury until 2014 about corruption and the need for a change in government did contribute to this end, but only partially—to the first part, Awesome Governance. The other three segments still need to be tackled.

Pushing for equality, a shift in societal values and the proper utilization of resources won't be easy, and the journey will be long. But I am excited. After all, how often do we get to be part of a generation that can actually fix the nation?

I do believe we can make India awesome by embracing a

fresh identity—by moving from our original positions as Self-focused Indifferent Indians or Caring but Aligned Indians, and growing into Caring Objective Indians. I believe we can achieve global eminence by remembering the lessons of the recent past—that no law or leader can solve our problems if *we* fail to display some initiative. I think we can dream of harmony and happiness if we celebrate the qualities that bind us as citizens, even while making allowances for differences. Most of all, if we understand the issues that confront India and help others understand them, we will have contributed to our common goal—making India one of the greatest countries on earth. The fact that you have picked up this book means that you share

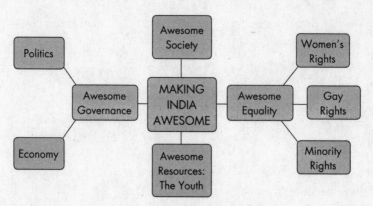

this goal with me and other readers.

I have one request. I never write an essay or discuss an Indian problem without proposing a solution, no matter how simple that resolution may sound. I urge you to do the same when you discuss a national issue anywhere. Let us not only complain and whine, but understand things and work them out.

Also, I am not perfect, nor are all my thoughts in every section in this book perfect. But let this book be a starting point. Let it generate more ideas about how we can turn our shared dream into a reality. Disagree with me, but at least have a point of view about the problem and a solution in mind. Do that, and in my eyes you will be what I call an awesome reader.

And when we will have enough awesome readers who care about our country, nothing can stop us from Making India Awesome!

Love,

Chetan Bhagat

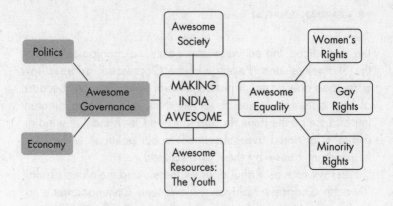

AWESOME GOVERNANCE: POLITICS AND ECONOMY

The cornerstone of any country, the control room containing the levers that manipulate the economy and society, is the government. In a democracy, the government is born out of politics. The kind of politics we have, the way voters think and the kind of people we elect to sit in the control room have a huge impact on the destiny of our nation.

Handling the levers of our country is what we call governance. It involves formulating and implementing policies, laws, rules and regulations to run our country. Unless we make this governance world class, there is no way our country can become awesome.

Hence, a lot of my writing revolves around politics and policies. Wherever possible, I try not to blame only the politicians. Politicians are replaceable. What is more important is what we, as voters, need to change about ourselves, in our everyday behaviour and thinking, to ensure that the people who enter the control room do indeed give us awesome governance.

In this section, 'Games Politicians Play' talks about how

the prejudiced Indian voter can easily be manipulated. 'We the Shameless' and 'Revenge of the Oppressed' address how corruption doesn't occur just because of politicians, but because of how different classes of society think and place a different importance on the issue. In 'The Kings in Our Minds', the Indian mentality of being over-subservient to our political leaders and its resultant abuse by them is discussed.

Essays such as 'Rahul's New Clothes, and the Naked Truth', 'Swachh Congress Abhiyan', 'Seventeen Commandments for Narendra Modi' and 'Analysing the Modi Effect' talk more directly of the dynamics of the main political parties in our nation.

Apart from politics, it is equally important to understand policies. My writings on 'The Telangana Effect' (on the division of Andhra Pradesh), 'Rescue the Nation' (on the role of the bureaucracy), 'Pro-poor or Pro-poverty?' (on the Food Security Bill), 'Can India's Backward Polity Provide a Pro-growth Economic Environment?' (on the state of the Indian economy), 'The Tiny-bang Theory for Setting Off Big-bang Reforms' (on the new government's cautious economic reforms) and 'To Make "Make in India" Happen, Delete Control' (on attracting foreign investments) talk about specific government policies, weighing in on the pros and cons of each.

Seventeen Commandments for Narendra Modi

> After a long time, we have had a stable mandate at the top. If the BJP blows this opportunity, it will set India back by a decade.

Let me forewarn you, dear reader—this is not going to be pretty. But, over a year after the Modi government came to power, it is important to take stock of what needs to be done.

Here is a list of seventeen action points if the Bharatiya Janata Party (BJP) wants to remain the dominant political party in India. After a long time, we have had a stable mandate at the top. If the BJP blows this opportunity, it will set India back by a decade. So, here goes.

- The prime minister, with all due respect, is floating too high. Come back to earth. Don't try to present an image of a global statesman. You won an anti-incumbency election when the Congress was weak, by increasing the BJP's vote share by a few percentage points. You have not transformed India yet. Don't be happy with just the applause from non-resident Indians (NRIs). If they love you so much, ask them to pay. If one lakh NRIs commit to paying the BJP $1,000 a year, that is a $100 million of clean money annually. Use that to clean up party funding. When are you going to do that anyway?

- Learn some valuable lessons from your trouncing in the Delhi elections in 2014. The results removed the halo around Modi, or ended the 'Modi wave'. They showed that the top leadership was clueless about the feelings of people on the street, or even their own party workers. They also cast doubt on Modi's ability to deliver on promises.

- Get the Lokpal Bill passed. Empower the Central Bureau of Investigation (CBI) and Central Vigilance Commission (CVC). Clean up corruption systemically. Don't say that if Modi is there, nobody can be corrupt. What if Modi isn't there tomorrow?

- Don't bully the media or juniors in the party. Inspire respect, not fear. Don't be smug. Don't kill talent in the party because it could be a threat to you one day. It's not in the BJP's DNA to be a one-man party.

- Shut up regressive Hindutva fanatics. We've heard them talk poisonous nonsense. You ignore them. They are your supporters. You have to tell them loud and clear this is not okay. The young generation doesn't find it cool to support a leader who doesn't believe in a free and equal society. Send some of your old-fashioned partymen abroad to learn about gender issues and minority rights. They will make you sink otherwise.

- Don't be overconfident in your speeches. Keep a circle of critics around you, not just those who keep singing 'Modiji is awesome'. Everything you utter in public must be pre-checked. A prime minister cannot be a rabble rouser.

- Dress down. Charisma comes from integrity, competence and compassion. Not from expensive clothes.

- Stay connected to, and do something visible, for the youth. They screamed for you in the Lok Sabha elections and filled their Twitter feeds and Facebook walls with your praises. What have you done for them? You went to Shri Ram

College of Commerce to give a speech before the elections. Have you visited any college after that? Why not? Are foreign visits more important?

- The party president may be really clever. But sometimes it isn't about who is the most clever but about who genuinely cares. Chess moves don't win elections all the time. A connect with people does. The party president, given his perceived persona (which may be at variance with who he really is), doesn't inspire confidence. You standing next to him is like Amitabh Bachchan standing next to Amar Singh. Did it help Mr Bachchan?

- Don't talk *down* to people. Talk *to* people. Don't address people if you never want to take questions. Don't give monologues on the radio. It reminds one of Indira Gandhi and North Korea. It's not cool. Do you really think a kid in Delhi University will tell his friends, 'Hey, can't miss that "Mann Ki Baat" on radio?'

- Open more colleges. Open up tourism. Reduce taxes on high-employment sectors. Give tax breaks for companies that move headquarters to smaller cities. Do anything to take skills and jobs to the interiors. Fix the primary schools. They have to teach well. Half our schoolkids can't read properly.

- The cities need extensions with very low-cost housing solutions, with good water, electricity and transport infrastructure. That is the only way the urban poor can live a life of dignity. Give them dignity. They didn't vote for you in Delhi, remember? Win them back.

- Be real. Have a work–life balance. Why can't the prime minister catch a movie sometimes? Or eat chaat in Delhi somewhere? A humanized prime minister works better than a glorified one.

- No statues, please. School or statue? Hospital or statue? No need to explain further.

- No personal attacks on opponents, no matter how punchy the joke or the temptation to say it. Again, run it past those critical advisers first.
- No hanging out with rich industrialists. Of course, you may need to officially. But it doesn't have to be a media event. Hang out with the billion people, not billionaires.

Finally, all of the above comes down to the party listening and acting according to the wishes of the people.

Games Politicians Play

> If a father buys his child toffees instead of books for school, it may make for a happy child. But does it make a good father?

Like certain flowers that blossom only in spring, Indian politics comes alive, and shows its true colours, during election time. The strategies adopted by political parties tell you what matters to people, or answer the elusive question—how exactly do Indians vote? Certain moves announced by political parties, whether absurd, controversial or unethical, provide you immense insight into what works for the average voter. Even the most rational, modern-thinking politicians adopt primitive and regressive measures in trying to pander to the electorate. They do this for one and only one purpose—to win. In fact, victory becomes so important that they forget, or ignore, the long-term repercussions of their actions on our society and nation as a whole. Whether it is taking in corrupt members only for the votes they can procure from their communities or announcing unrealistic freebies or quotas on the basis of caste or religion, politics becomes a circus at the time of elections.

If a father buys his child toffees instead of books for school, it may make for a happy child. But does it make a good father?

For a change, I am not blaming any of the politicians for such actions. If we were in the same situation, perhaps we too would be left with no choice but to adopt similar measures. The problem is not with the politicians, who simply mirror and adapt to the environment. The issue is with the Indian electorate, or us. The great Indian mind is filled with prejudice. Centuries of persecution and discrimination—even in the present day—on the one hand and a belief in the superiority of one's own kind on the other, have led to these prejudices. These in turn have led to a haphazard democracy—more cacophony than consensus. The ruckus that we often see in Parliament is nothing but a visualization of the average Indian mind, of chaos and confusion about who we really are. Even the most educated of us are prejudiced. One simple test of prejudice is this—will you allow your siblings or children to marry outside your community or religion? If your answer is no, then no matter how much you cheer for the Indian team, stand at attention for the national anthem or cheer the Indian flag, you are prejudiced. And as long as most of us stay prejudiced, we will have the confused and mediocre leadership that we have right now. No matter how many fasts activists undertake or good policies economists suggest, if we don't get the concept of being Indian in our heads and treat that above anything else, we will remain a messed-up country.

Yes, Dalits were treated badly in the past, and some still suffer. Muslims were—and some of them still are—discriminated against. However, things have improved. If you shed your prejudices, they will improve even faster.

If there were no prejudices, there would be no need for political parties to play the caste card or to announce quotas within quotas.

If we don't change, however, we are moving towards disaster. There will be lack of decision-making, inefficiency and a stalling of progress and growth in our country. The young generation will find it even more difficult to get a good education and well-paid jobs. After all, if we choose our leader based only on the toffees he gives us, then we somewhat deserve our fate.

Revenge of the Oppressed: Why Corruption Continues to Be Around Despite the Outcry Against It

> Everybody wants to remove corruption. However, not every Indian feels it is the number one priority.

From speaking engagements to dinner with friends, one question is constant: why isn't corruption going away? The question baffles the educated middle classes. Why is a reasonable, universal and noble demand for an honest society so difficult to achieve in a democracy? And why is it that corrupt parties win elections time and time again?

Frustrated, the educated middle class comes up with elitist theories like '90 per cent of Indians are stupid' or 'most voters are dumb'. None of this is true. The Indian voter is rational. However, he is rational within his own framework. It is important to grasp the demographics and social context of Indian voters.

Sure, at one level everybody wants to remove corruption. Every Indian would like a clean society. However, not every Indian feels it is the number one priority. For a lot of Indians, corruption doesn't determine their voting behaviour. Removing corruption is important to them. However, it is not as important as, say, (a) one's identity; (b) their safety; and (c) obtaining some instant gratification from politicians during voting time.

Clever politicians understand this. They work to deliver on these priorities and, in return, are allowed to be corrupt by the voters. This often occurs amongst the section of voters that has historically been oppressed or sees itself as a subjugated minority.

Of course, this is an oversimplified generalization. The situation is changing. For there are Muslim voters or lower-caste voters or low-income voters who want corruption removed more than anything else. However, a lot of Muslims also vote to feel safe (hence they may avoid voting for the BJP). Many low-income voters would rather have 'bird-in-hand freebies' at election time (as later on the politician will forget them—a completely rational view). Similarly, many lower-caste voters may feel happy to see their community's candidate in power, as it makes life seem a little fairer after generations of oppression.

With such conflicting agendas, the issue of corruption gets clouded. Voting patterns do show corruption as a variable (hence ministers step down). However, it is not the top influencer yet. Thus, a corrupt party can enjoy power as long as it keeps the oppressed classes happy and can play Robin Hood to them. Every party knows this; thus, every party is corrupt, though to varying degrees.

In some ways, the stickiness of corruption is the revenge of the oppressed. It is we, the educated, usually upper-class, upper-caste Hindus, who are empowered enough to have higher-order needs of an honest and fair society. The oppressed won't let us have it just yet. They do want to remove corruption, but they also want certain injustices fixed and other scores settled. For this, they send agents to power who might loot the nation, but protect them and even share the booty through the occasional handout.

It isn't fair to today's youth, who want a corruption-free India to maximize opportunities above anything else. However, there were centuries of unfairness that the oppressed had to bear too.

Will it ever change? Yes. It has to change because plunder and redistribution is a highly inefficient model for societal fairness. We are a poor country. There isn't much to plunder anyway. The solution lies in setting aside differences for a while. The upper-caste, upper-class Hindus have to let go of their bigotry and prejudice. The oppressed have to let go of their justified but expensive urge for revenge and retribution. All over the world, the oppressed have only risen through self-empowerment—look at the Jews and the Parsis. Oppressed community voters are realizing that many of their current representatives have harmed the nation, filled their own pockets and done little for them.

We are not a nation of stupid voters. We are simply a nation where people want different things, and that's okay. However, removing corruption will require it to be made the number one priority for all Indians. It is a secular issue, and removing it will be beneficial to all.

When the roof of the house is leaky, you need to fix the roof first rather than fight family feuds. We do become one during cricket matches, and we did win the World Cup in 2011. If we can become one on this issue of fighting corruption, we will be able to win against it as well.

Game for it?

We the Shameless

It's time to stop blaming just our politicians for corruption and look within.

Time and time again, we have seen our political parties defend their corrupt members and even back them for important posts. Their first standard excuse is 'nothing malafide is proven yet'. The second classic excuse is 'look at what other parties have done'. Therefore, a murderer can be spared, as long as he can find another murderer.

It is important to understand why all political parties back their corrupt members, despite massive allegations and enough circumstantial evidence against such people. The answer lies in the way Indians think. While it is easy to blame politicians, the fact remains that our politicians are not ethical because we aren't ethical. A large number of politicians have lost track of the idea that every profession in this world has ethics—it may not be illegal to break them but still is definitely wrong. A doctor must treat his patient as soon as possible, it is assumed, under ethical medical practice. But if he delays treatment, it would be hard to prove it illegal. A teacher must try to teach her students well, though if she doesn't, it won't be illegal. Society needs ethics as much as laws to function well.

The simple, bitter truth is that the electorate just doesn't care much about financial impropriety. Sure, we bicker, moan and fuss about politicians looting us. However, it is not that high up in the hierarchy of wrongs a politician could commit. A moderate amount of corruption is almost expected and accepted. It is only when graft is done in an obvious large-scale and arrogant manner that Indians get somewhat upset—and that too for a short period of time. 'Do it, but don't be so blatant and rub it in our faces,' is what we seem to be telling them.

Tax evasion, dubious accounting and shady friendships are almost seen as natural behaviour for an Indian businessman. We don't see them as crimes. We treat them on a par with, say, eating four plates of dessert—a bit greedy, but understandable.

Until we, as a society, really feel that graft, unethical behaviour and nepotism are huge problems, and start to truly care about all of them, politicians will not change.

Take, for instance, a hypothetical situation. Say, a prominent politician went into a temple with his shoes on, with a bottle of alcohol and kicked the idols. What would happen? Of course, there would be huge societal outrage. In our value system, we hold our religious shrines extremely dear. Such a person would never be allowed to remain party president. In all probability, the person's political career would end overnight.

But this value system does not apply when we see shady businesses being conducted, state coffers being looted or politicians placing self-interest above national interest. Even abuse of power is something we only talk about in public. Deep down, we are complicit. We may want political leaders to not abuse power, but do so ourselves. Just take one example, the status of domestic help in India. How do Indians treat their domestic help? Why don't we ever talk about a minimum wage for them? Or perhaps a compulsory day off every week? When we ourselves have no qualms abusing our power, it is difficult to attack others for doing so.

We, the Indian society, need to reflect on who we have become. Organizations like the Rashtriya Swayamsevak Sangh (RSS), which claim to care for India's glory, should be fixing this by propagating good values in society. And parties which claim removal of corruption as their topmost agenda, like the Aam Aadmi Party (AAP), should also send out the message that it is a lack of values within us, and not just a few bad guys at the top, that has turned India corrupt.

More than anything, we ourselves must change, and see the sense in doing so. A society without values cannot survive or function, let alone progress. When this realization dawns on a larger section of society, politicians will change. The BJP might fire Nitin Gadkari and the Congress might create an uproar to take action against Robert Vadra.

Right now, they don't, because they think you, the voter, doesn't care. That you will see Gadkari's punishment as a slight to the RSS, or to the community or caste he belongs to. Similarly, no Congressman will stand up for what is right in Vadra's case, as the Congress voter cares for the Gandhi family more than for right or wrong.

We live in shameless times. When long-overdue self-reflection and shame strike us, India will be ready for change. We have seen many exposés on corrupt leaders in the past few years; it is time we did an exposé on ourselves.

The Kings in Our Minds

Kings and colonizers left our country nearly seven decades ago. It is time they left our minds.

I remember one afternoon when there was a traffic jam on the Western Express Highway in Mumbai. This vital suburban highway connects various important points of the city, including the airport. I, like several others on the road, had a flight to catch. On a normal day, it would have taken ten minutes to the terminal. However, that day, the traffic had not moved for over half an hour.

The jam wasn't due to road construction or a vehicle mishap. Instead, a few cops had intentionally stopped the traffic. 'VIP movement,' is all a cop told me when I asked. Some of us begged the cops to let us pass, lest we miss our flight. The cops shooed us away. The stranded crowd smirked at us, as if saying how stupid of us to even try.

I saw the faces of people waiting on their bikes, in cars, buses and autorickshaws. The long jam meant literally thousands of people waiting to move behind us. People were late for work, business meetings, doctor's appointments, social visits and college. Yet, while everyone was uncomfortable, nobody seemed agitated either. After all, this was a part of Indian life. A neta passes, the world around has to stop.

I made frantic calls to the airline staff and managed to get a boarding pass printed. When traffic finally cleared, I was lucky to make it to the flight. The airline, aware of the jam, had delayed the plane somewhat. It would now delay other flights elsewhere in India. Despite this, many passengers couldn't make it. These people spent considerable time, effort and money to rebook themselves to their destinations. I had a speaking engagement in my destination city. If I had missed this flight, the function would have had to be cancelled.

Meanwhile, I assume the neta arrived in Mumbai, had people salute him, lift his bags and shut his car doors. He would have zipped off on the highway, on his way to cut a ribbon somewhere or for a meeting; probably important but not terribly urgent either. If the road had not been cleared for him, he would have still reached his destination, perhaps ten minutes later (and with a more realistic picture of the roads and traffic in Mumbai). However, to ensure his comfort, thousands waited for an hour, airlines upset schedules and at least one event planner in the country had a panic attack.

Who was this VIP? He was a member of Parliament, a minister. He was neither the king of India nor the colonial ruler of our country. We don't have those anymore. The person was an elected representative, someone people had chosen to do a job. Sure, to handle a ministry of a large country is not a small job. He does deserve respect for it. However, does respect mean subservience? If someone has a powerful job, does that mean we accept any form of power abuse from him or her? Do we think it is okay for a busy city to stop just because some elected leader needs a smooth ride to his or her meeting? If we do, aren't we at some level accepting, and even becoming accomplices in, the subjugation?

Of course, some would argue: what other option do we have? Creating a ruckus on the jammed road would only create more havoc. A public protest could turn into a mob-like situation, which isn't the solution either. The answer to power abuse is not anarchy.

So what do we do? Before we answer that, we need to see why our elected representatives continue to think of themselves as little monarchs.

Our political class inherited a British colonial system, which had zero accountability to the colonized. Quite cleverly, they didn't change laws to bring in accountability, the cornerstone of any democracy. Till date, our netas try to rule us like colonial rulers and hate any proposals that reduce their powers or demand accountability. No wonder the Jan Lokpal Bill hasn't yet been passed!

While such legal and policy battles continue, a large part of the problem is also the Indian mindset. We do see them as our kings. We do think that 'they are in power' means 'they can do anything'. We do not realize that 'being in power' means 'being in power only to do things in the national interest'.

If Indians change this mindset, changes to laws and policies will follow. Specifically, if a majority of us see and expect netas to be service providers instead of rulers, it will trigger a huge behavioural change in the political class.

How do you change mindsets across the country? Well, start with yourself, and then try to change as many others as possible. If you suffer, talk about it. Text friends, talk about it on social networks and to your colleagues. Tell everyone if you witness abuse of power, especially when your service provider neta acts like an entitled prince. Sure, they drive your nation, but just as a hired driver drives a bus. The driver cannot start believing he owns the bus. The driver should also know that if he doesn't drive well, he will be removed.

So let us work on changing this mindset if we want a better India. Kings and colonizers left our country nearly seven decades ago. It is time they left our minds.

The Telangana Effect

> The answer to India's problems is not a new state.
> It may be, rather, a new state of mind.

An endearing, almost cute trait of Indians is that we never really lose hope. We always feel that a messiah or a great grand scheme will soon come and deliver us from our woes. It is a narrative reinforced by Bollywood, where somehow a hero works things out in the end. Our mythology, too, talks about good forces (God) with amazing powers coming and killing the evil ones (demons).

It is perhaps due to this gullibility that many of us feel that the sure-shot solution to the miserable common man's life in India is a new state.

Yes, 'stateitis' is the new virus in town, affecting everyone from the south to the east to the north. So, what is the latest solution for the common man's suffering? A new state. Not good leaders, not even new leaders, not new criteria for voting—such as governance over caste—not an end to identity prejudice.

We will change none of this. We will simply solve all our employment, inflation, power, water, safety, health and education problems with one magic solution—a new state. If the consequences of such naïve thinking weren't serious, it would be another cute, hilarious trait of Indians. However, what we started with Telangana is something so harmful, vile and terrible, we will all regret it in times to come if we don't check it now. And that terrible thing is this: making states at gunpoint.

No, making new states is not a problem. In the right circumstances, it may well help. What creates problems are coercive demands for a state, where sections of the population threaten violence or strikes and try to gouge out a state for themselves.

However, if we want to stem such movements, it won't be through forcibly shutting them down. It is important to understand where such demands originate, and if something can be done to address the underlying issues without constantly redrawing the map of the country.

So, why the almost sudden desire for so many new states? Well, the demand seems to be coming from the more economically backward pockets of the country. The simple reason is this: people are sick of poor governance and don't know where to look for answers or place the blame. A new state, even if a flawed idea, seems like something new to try.

Also, Indians are prejudiced, aiding such thought. Many of us Indians feel our community/religion/caste is somehow superior to others'. We also feel a leader from our own kind will have more empathy towards us. Hence, a new state seems like a reasonable solution.

Of course, this is highly flawed thinking. For our prejudice itself is often the reason behind our woes. If we were not prejudiced, we would not have voted on the basis of identity. We would have chosen instead a leader based on ability. We didn't, which in turn led to the governance mess we find ourselves in today.

This bitter truth, of course, doesn't cut much ice with us Indians. We never buy stories involving us taking responsibility. We never blame ourselves. It is always an external demon, and usually from another caste/community/religion, that causes our woes. Not us.

Unfortunately, caught amidst our desperate life situations and prejudiced minds, we forget the damage pseudo-fixes like new states may cause. For, no matter what your local leader may tell you about the utopia that will come after making a new state, there are many drawbacks. Here are four.

First, small states have little clout at the centre. Let's face it, the chief minister of Uttar Pradesh carries more clout than his counterpart in Tripura. Size matters in politics.

Two, it creates separatist, almost anti-national sentiments that are harmful for the country. There were reports of people in Telangana being asked to move out of the new state. If new states are created in Assam or West Bengal, there could be violence. Indians living peacefully for generations could become adversaries overnight. How can this be good for the country?

Three, business investors are likely to stay away from a newly formed state, especially if the state is created under volatile circumstances. This will mean fewer new jobs and a worse-off situation for the new state. Frankly, without investments, no backward area can develop. Politicians may yield to shrill voices, investors will run away from them.

Four, it reinforces and almost validates something we Indians should be ashamed of—our internal prejudices.

Today, the world is looking at India to get its act together. We, on the other hand, are busy finding differences and reasons to hate each other. Andhra Pradesh was a wonderful state by itself. Sure, it may have had issues like any other. Cutting it up, making many parts of India vulnerable and legitimizing prejudice hardly seems like a smart solution.

There's nothing wrong with making a few new states, but it has to be done on the right terms. The intent has to be rational and the process objective and peaceful. The reason for making states should be administrative and not indulging prejudices. The answer to India's problems is not a new state. It may be, rather, a new state of mind. A modern, unprejudiced, thinking Indian mind. Can we add that to the list of new state demands please?

Analysing the Modi Effect

> Figuring Modi out gives us insights into who we are as Indians.

Few politicians are as fascinating as Narendra Modi. And for nearly a decade and a half, no politician has been as controversial. Neither has any politician been accused, blacklisted, vilified and treated like a pariah as much. Yet he has not only survived, but thrived.

It has been over a year since Modi won the 2014 Lok Sabha elections. What's amazing is that the criticism has not stopped even as the Godhra riots' censure has subsided.

Anyhow, one thing is clear—Modi's political graph has continued to rise. Even the always-righteous-but-not-always-right Arvind Kejriwal, who has successfully tarnished many reputations so far—Nitin Gadkari, Robert Vadra, Mukesh Ambani, Sheila Dikshit, to name a few—has been unable to really puncture the Modi effect. As he enters his second year in office, Modi's popularity has not nose-dived, as so often happens with politicians who are voted into office with landslide majorities by voters who think that these leaders are their new messiahs.

Why is that so? Is it just Modi's development agenda? Is it a lack of choice? Is it Modi's personality and oratory? Or is it his never-overstated-yet-always-present Hindutva stance? Other BJP leaders have run states well—Manohar Parrikar and Shivraj Singh Chouhan, for instance. So why does Modi command a wild and passionate fan base like no other BJP leader?

Answering these questions is important.

First, understanding Modi's popularity is important for his opposition. For now, opponents seem to be helping Modi more than hurting him. Criticism is Modi's polish, making him shine even more.

Second, figuring Modi out gives us insights into who we are as Indians.

An aspect mostly overlooked about Indian society is its understated, often subdued but strong sense of Hindu entitlement. Sure, our Constitution and laws are secular. Our public discourse shuns communal arguments, and rightly so. However, this doesn't mean the sense of entitlement goes away.

With an over 80 per cent Hindu population, comprising the majority of the world's Hindus, it is nearly impossible to eliminate that sense of majority entitlement. Add to that the Congress's strategy of turning Muslims into a vote bank and responding better to Muslim issues. This triggered the Hindu sense of dissatisfaction even more.

In this context, a leader representing Hindu pride found resonance. This is why many people do not ascribe much importance to the handling of post-Godhra riots when it comes to judging Modi. For one, his role wasn't clear (and hasn't legally been proven). Second, to a section of people it felt like retribution.

Of course, this ignores the fact that the Muslims who allegedly burnt the train or organized terror attacks had nothing to do with the Muslims who suffered during the riots. However, emotions often supersede reason and a disgruntled Hindu populace has mostly pardoned Modi. Again, I make no judgement whether this was right or wrong, but this is what has happened.

Third, the reason why Modi did well is his ability to manage expectations. He worked in Gujarat until it showed at least some good metrics. More importantly, Modi never made tall claims beforehand. He worked hard first and marketed himself later.

Fourth, his personality is the exact opposite of Manmohan Singh's. Modi is a straight talker and people like that. They want a prime minister who has opinions, even if they are not the most polished. It doesn't hurt that Modi has a sense of humour. Humour creates connect and adds charm.

Five, Modi represents practicality. Most Indians know that while it is good to remove corruption, nepotism, dynasty, oppression of women and a million other wrongs, it isn't easy. Things change, but slowly and over time. The leader many Indians seek is not idealistic, but someone who can do a fairly good job despite the muck in our society.

Finally, Modi was, plain and simple, lucky. Rahul Gandhi was weak as a major opponent. The scam-ridden United Progressive Alliance (UPA) decade had upset most Indians. The arrogance of Congress leaders didn't help either. Modi arrived at a time when people wanted change.

It could be luck. Or, as they say in Hindu terms, it might just be destiny.

Can India's Backward Polity Provide a Pro-growth Economic Environment?

> We were, and to some extent still are, in the middle of an economic crisis.

About a decade ago, enthusiastic investment bankers and financial research analysts were tom-tomming the India growth story. India, they said, had so much potential, it could be one of the world's biggest economies in the next couple of decades. For this, they used spreadsheet models, in which they plugged in a growth rate of 8–10 per cent and projected it for the next thirty years. They learnt this in business schools.

Of course, anything growing at a compound annual rate of 10 per cent will become pretty massive in thirty years (17.4 times, to be precise). Hence, the sharp minds made an earth-shattering prediction: that anything growing very fast will become very big over time. Clients of financial institutions, seduced by such a rosy picture about the land of miracles, bought into the idea.

The boring economies of Europe, growing at 1–2 per cent, just didn't carry the spiciness of India. Billions came into India, and the sudden rush of money did lead to some growth. The government in power took the entire credit for it. 'We have created growth,' the government spokesperson used to say. The party had started.

The analysts were rewarded and flushed with heavy bonuses at the end of the year. Young mergers and acquisitions bankers bought apartments with a slum-and-racecourse view or a slum-and-sea view in Mumbai. Of course, the idea was to ignore the slum and focus on the sea view or the racecourse.

In all this, a few uncomfortable questions were never asked. For instance, was the then government committed to providing a pro-business, pro-growth economic environment? Was the Indian polity ready to accept this new capitalist system? Are we socialist or are we market-driven? Could we actually grow so fast every year, considering that each power plant or new road or mining approval takes years? Are we efficient manufacturers for the world? Are our taxation and regulations in line with fast growth requirements? Do we have an educated or skilled workforce to grow average incomes seventeen times in the next thirty years? Is our infrastructure in place?

No, no and no. But you don't ask these questions when there is a good party in progress. You sound like the neighbourhood uncle who crashes a party and demands that the music be turned down. Naysayers are seen to be jealous, doomsday mongers who can't bear to see India come into its own.

Of course, with none of the fundamentals required for such massive growth in place, the money coming into the country had little to do. Sure, a few projects did take off, and the first few companies that arrived did find their products selling well, given the pent-up demand. However, soon, growth petered out.

The government had, of course, used this temporary growth phase to start its own mini-party. Budgets showed higher revenue but even higher spending. The government spent way more than it earned. Consequently, private players faced interest rates of 15 per cent for borrowings. The government printed so many rupees, it flooded the market and the currency bought less and less.

All this was going on behind the scenes, while growth numbers were good. Hence, all was forgiven. Media analyses of the budgets included the finance minister's sartorial tastes and the couplets he recited in his speech. Everybody was happy in wonderland.

Of course, soon the penny dropped. People never saw returns for their money and stopped investing. Dollars stopped coming to India. Local players took their money out too. Growth slowed and the government blamed the media, the opposition, the foreigners and even the middle class for it. At the same time, it spent even more, further increasing borrowing costs and inflation.

One day, the party ended. People figured it was a bubble. Reality is more than just a growth-rate formula in a spreadsheet. A socialist country cannot turn market-friendly overnight. A corrupt nation cannot be competitive in the world. A divided population cannot arrive at decisions fast. A nation cannot decide to welcome investors one year, but pull a fast one on them the next year.

We were, and to some extent still are, whether the government likes to admit it or not, in the middle of an economic crisis. We have seen many companies go bust, large lay-offs, massive inflation and high unemployment. The reforms initiated by the new government have brought some relief, but the crisis is far from over.

The economic numbers were bad enough; but they also led to something much worse—a crisis of confidence. The same analysts who were celebrating India a few years ago told their clients to avoid India and its unreliable regime. If the world stops trusting India, this trust will take years to rebuild. This is why Prime Minister Narendra Modi launched the 'Make in India' campaign, to instil trust among foreign investors again and encourage foreign companies to manufacture in India. It has worked to some extent, as the last economic survey by chief economic adviser Arvind Subramaniam projects an 8 per cent growth for 2016.* For this, India needs to rein in its expenditure and fiscal deficit, and focus on public investment.

Forget growing seventeen times in thirty years, but hopefully, the reforms initiated by the new government will pull the country out of the crisis it was heading into. Otherwise, the future of an entire generation is at stake. And yes, next time, don't ignore the slum view while taking in the sea view.

*http://economictimes.indiatimes.com/news/economy/indicators/ economic-survey-2015-india-headed-for-8-plus-growth-in-2016-says-arvind-subramanian/articleshow/46403068.cms

Rahul's New Clothes, and the Naked Truth

> If there is a new Rahul possible,
> we need to see him, and soon.

In school, I remember taking part in a play called *The Emperor's New Clothes*. The plot revolved around a king who was tricked into believing that he was wearing a special outfit, when in fact he was naked. His sycophants complimented him for his wonderful choice of clothing. When the emperor went out on the street, scared commoners praised the invisible suit. Finally, an innocent little kid screamed: 'Look, the emperor has no clothes!'

That one loud comment sent the entire town into shock. However, since it was the truth, nobody could deny it anymore. And eventually, the emperor came back to his senses.

The Congress desperately needs that kid. Someone, perhaps, who could stand up at an All India Congress Committee (AICC) national convention and shout: 'Look, Rahul Gandhi is not working at all!'

One can almost predict the silence in the auditorium thereafter, akin to the silence in the town square. The first reaction would be denial, or even attacking the person who said it. Better still, labelling him elitist, biased, paid, bigoted, idiot, evil, ignorant or any other negative adjective that comes to mind. However, as the Enrique Iglesias song goes—'You can run, you can hide, but you can't escape my love' (in this case, the truth).

This truth is particularly bitter because the Congress has little idea about how to fix the problem. As many say, if the family doesn't work, what is the Congress? Right now, the party hasn't done much besides cashing in on the Gandhi family's legacy. In fact, it has used the family name to hide incompetence and even abused it to cover up scams. The family brand is so depleted that there isn't much legacy left anymore.

Whether it was rampant corruption, record inflation or the latest, the safety of citizens—the Gandhis did not answer any questions. This riled the educated middle classes. The Gandhis hardly ever took questions, in public or in the media. Rahul Gandhi gave his first TV interview as late as January 2014. They still address political rallies with well-rehearsed speeches. There are no interactive sessions or audience questions. The rare press conference is stage-managed, with answers that often deflect the issues and no counter-questioning allowed. People expect rapid, direct, relevant and heartfelt communication from people in charge. These expectations rise in times of crises, which the nation had seen aplenty during Congress rule. The people wanted the family to talk—not spokespersons, agents, sycophants or trained deflectors. They also wanted the family to speak with sincerity and what they truly feel, not read from rehearsed scripts. This is why Prime Minister Manmohan Singh's relatively harmless 'theek hai' in 2012 caused so much outrage. It cemented the belief that the prime minister didn't speak from the heart.

It was not inflation, corruption or even lack of safety that ultimately brought the Congress down. What made people lose faith is this silence, which came across as a mix of smug arrogance, incompetence and lack of compassion. This silence once meant restraint and poise. Later, it was seen as insensitive.

The young generation doesn't know what to make of them. Should they associate the Gandhi family with sacrifice, or see them as people who keep silent and help cover up corruption? Are the Gandhis interested in making Indian lives better, or are they merely self-preservers? What is the answer? It is all a big confusing mess, and youngsters see no reason why the surname means that the party deserves their vote. The results are there for all to see.

The bigger issue is: how to restore the legacy? Well, when a legacy has been destroyed, you either restore it, or build a new one. It will serve the Congress better if it does both. One, it needs to restore the Gandhi family's pride. For this, they have to become relevant to the times. The world has changed. The silent treatment just doesn't work with people in the digitally connected world. Social networks, multiple TV channels, mobile phone updates are tools that didn't exist in India two decades ago. Their penetration will continue to grow in the coming few years. The overload of media, connectivity and content means scrutiny levels are way higher than before. Integrity can no longer be feigned. Clever words, or even calculated silences, if faked, backfire.

If there is one thing the Congress party should, and could easily change, it is to get the Gandhis to talk—not just read out speeches, but engage, interact and respond to questions and concerns.

It's simply the new reality of Indian politics. The fact is that if Rahul starts engaging with the people, the Congress can regain a lot of the lost trust.

But Rahul doesn't have to only *talk* about being honest and caring; he has to *become* honest and caring. If there is a new Rahul possible, we need to see him, and soon. He needs to apologize for hiding when the nation needed him. He has to show he cares for India. No glibness, no cleverness, no attempts to say something deep and profound. He has to say sorry for not acting when he needed to. For trying to be too clever and keeping mum (no pun intended) during scams. For claiming to be a youth leader but letting youth down. For posing as a messiah of the downtrodden, but only using them to secure a caste-based vote bank. These tricks, possibly handed down to him over the generations, do not work in the Internet age. Sincerity, or the lack of it, can be spotted. Frankly, he not only has to become a good politician, but also a good human being. In the current climate—goodness is the new cool. He needs to talk, give more and better interviews, get shamed even, but plough through it all and deliver despite that. While leaders do not look good apologizing, if coupled with firings, it will have a positive effect. However, if the apology is stage-managed, especially with some clever uncle guiding the proceedings behind the scenes, it will backfire.

On the subject of firings—senior people need to be publicly humiliated and fired in the Congress, not those who lost an election, but those who destroyed the legacy.

The Gandhis of today need to own up to mess-ups and mistakes. Rahul needs to talk regularly and take questions from the people and the media. Yes, this would mean more criticism, misinterpretations and perhaps even slander. Yes, actions matter far more than talk. However, communicating with people will show his openness and willingness to take feedback. It will show that in his heart he cares for the people. He and the Gandhi family have to become the 'ideals' for the nation. Are they up for it?

This is not an easy task, but not impossible either. The Gandhis have lost trust amongst many. They need to win it back. The bigger issue is, does the Congress want to rebuild itself? More than anything, does the emperor have the courage to listen to the kid who is right?

Swachh Congress Abhiyan: Some Essential Steps

> Since the Congress and the BJP are the only two plausible national alternatives right now, we must keep things competitive between them.

The Congress used to project itself as the perfect party led by a wonderful family that could do no wrong. After all, it had remained in power longer than anyone else.

But it is also a party where nobody opens their mouth, even if the emperor has no clothes on. The members deliver pre-rehearsed messages, which glorify the Gandhi family and bash all opposition. Hardly any Congress party member speaks his mind, or comes across as having any sense of personal conviction. Ask him a question about the Gandhi family and he freezes. It is understandable. A Congressperson's nightmare is the first family being upset with him or her. An ex-chief minister confessed to me once how a mere stern look from Sonia Gandhi could cause him nightmares for weeks. For, if you fall into her bad books, decades of hard work come to nothing. In 2014, a Congress minister was suspended for criticizing Rahul Gandhi. Thus, any career-conscious Congressperson would always ingratiate himself/herself with the family.

This nice, happy arrangement worked till 2014. The set-up operated because of one thing—the absolute charisma of the Gandhi family. Put them in front of Indians and they would, almost by reflex, vote for the Congress. Such a magic-wand family was priceless. You could be inept, corrupt, arrogant, inaccessible, but come election day, one flashing smile from the family, and the votes would come pouring in.

However, that is not the case anymore. The first family cannot help the Congress party win elections. In fact, they could not even make their party win in their own constituencies of Amethi and Rae Bareli in 2012, or even one seat during the 2014 Delhi elections. And of course, their loss at the national stage has been much talked about. These shocking and significant developments will cause a permanent, tectonic shift in Indian politics.

Does that mean all hope is lost for the Congress? Not really. It can readjust, but that would take a major restructuring within the party, including taking some decisions that were unmentionable a few years ago. But first, let us see what has led to this situation. Rahul Gandhi, seen as the ultimate youth leader some years ago, is unable to win elections for the party. In fact, wherever he is involved, the party loses miserably. Why?

The most important reason is the rise of regional stars, fuelled by the electorate's need for a leader who will understand local issues. India is truly turning federal now, where people look to their state chief ministers for progress and meeting their needs. People want their own local star chief minister. This is mainly because India is large and diverse. The issues in Kerala are different from those in Chhattisgarh. The Congress, with its culture of sycophancy and hoarding power at the top, was deeply ineffective in making local stars, particularly in big states.

Second, the Congress kept such a weak prime minister for the last decade that people lost faith in that position till Modi came to power. The Congress prime minister was akin to our president, more a ceremonial position. By demeaning the prime minister's post, the Congress brought this upon itself.

Of course, other issues like corruption have also made a dent, but more than the corruption, its arrogance and lack of repentance irritated voters. The first family, or the prime minister, never talked to the media. Neither did they instil confidence in the party's set of values. There didn't seem to be any moral compass guiding the party. It was all about stage management, the underlying assumption being people are fools, and somehow we have to wing it in elections with gimmicks like quotas. The prime minister should have resigned over such massive scams as the 2G and coal block. The first family should have apologized to the people for violating their trust. Yet, they continued to pretend that everything was normal and shielded the corrupt, hoping the issue would pass. Can the quest for an honest society based on good values ever pass? Who were they fooling but themselves? Today, thus, they are in a situation where the family has lost credibility.

But before writing on reviving the Congress, one must answer the moral question—should the Congress be revived at all? Is it more in India's interest to let it flounder and die, because the party's past sins can never be forgiven, and we have a decent government in place anyway? Or is it necessary in a democracy to have at least two strong national alternatives, which in turn creates competition and keeps politicians on their toes?

Both arguments have validity. The Congress's arrogance, scams and insistence on dynasty despite the country rejecting its heirs makes one wonder: why should one bother at all? Let it stew in its own mess; what could be better retribution for repeatedly ignoring the people who gave it power?

Well, there are reasons for fixing the Congress. One, a healthy and reasonably strong opposition is only good for a democracy. In fact, even the BJP could suffer if the Congress is too weak. Lack of accountability is what has led to problems in the past. If we kill all competition for the ruling party, I don't see how we will bring out the best in the government. For it is when politicians fear no competition that they become smug and arrogant and make irreparable mistakes. Since the Congress and the BJP are the only two plausible national alternatives right now, we must keep things competitive between them, rather than make any one party feel indispensable or invincible. Also, we must understand—political parties are amorphous, dynamic organizations that change over time. The mandir-loving BJP of the 1980s, for instance, is different from the present-day BJP. Citizens can and should hammer parties into the right shape. The Congress is no exception.

So what should be done? The number one issue, of course, is leadership and the role of the Gandhi family. The issue is perplexing because the Gandhi family serves two purposes at the top. One, it is a nationally known brand. With a legacy and history, the Gandhis are the face of the Congress. Two, they hold the party together. If they leave, there would be a mad scramble for the throne, creating a risk of implosion and chaos.

The first purpose—the Gandhis as a selling point—no longer holds. They bring limited value in terms of winning elections. Whatever few seats the Congress wins now are usually due to the appeal of the local leader. In fact, the bitter truth is that the brand may even have negative effect. At the moment, Rahul Gandhi is a vote-cutter, not a vote-getter. Many Indians hold the view that he is either incapable, or not interested, or doesn't quite get us. It could all be a huge misunderstanding, with Rahul's inherent genius lost on commoners, but perceptions matter in politics.

The second purpose is tricky. The Gandhis are still needed as the power glue at the top. Which is why confused Congressmen want to replace Rahul, but only with another Gandhi. Sadly, even Priyanka may not work, with little experience, inclination or capability demonstrated so far. What then, Congressmen?

Well, replacing Rahul with Priyanka is not the answer. More than anything, if the Congress or, for that matter, any national party wants to stay relevant and in sync with the people, it has to change the power order within the party. It simply has to turn into a manager of local stars, rather than having one family shine at the top.

In order to be solution-oriented and not rub salt in wounds, here is a quick five-step solution to get the revival started in the Congress. It's drastic, unspoken but needed. Well, someone needs to bell the cat, so here goes:

1. Create a triumvirate of power: Three young Congress leaders hold potential in terms of their capability as well as brand recognition. Sachin Pilot, Milind Deora and Jyotiraditya Scindia are somewhat known and seen as the newer avatar of the Congress. Control must be handed over to them, and between themselves they can carve out roles for each other. Since real power is a while away, there won't be a need to choose the super boss amongst the three for a long time.

2. Graceful handover of power: The trick is to not come across as though the family has been toppled. The triumvirate should not go head-on against the family in party elections. Rahul needs to feel more secure and adopt a more collaborative style, not be the sole and final voice on every issue, but have his team do it. He himself must anoint the three as heads of the party, with full freedom to run the show. Rahul need not himself exit. He can play the role of a moral conscience-keeper, speaking when needed from the margins and on high-level conceptual issues, which seems to be to his liking anyway. In fact, the role of the entire Gandhi family must change. It should work out a gradual, phase-wise schedule of handing over power to people down

below—Congressmen who actually do the work and deserve to be the leaders. The family's best bet in the future is to remain as the moral compass of the party, enforcing good values and throwing out people who don't adhere to them. It should not become a spent force shielding the corrupt, campaigning non-stop or trying to hoard power.

3. Weed out the unnecessary: If party members are old, rusted and tarnished, there is no reason to keep them. If Modi can have the courage to remove ministers, who were tall leaders themselves, in five months, the triumvirate can definitely do some weeding out (with Rahul's tacit blessing). The Congress needs to publicly fire some party heavyweights. Many of their senior leaders had become the face of the party's arrogance and corruption, at least in perception if not reality. They will probably never win another election and if they stick around, they won't let others win too. Since politics is about keeping only the useful, the Congress should make a huge show of humiliating these people and showing them the door. Of course, the family will enjoy a permanent immunity card, just as popular celebrities are never evicted early from a reality show. But the rest, well, you know what they say about horses and usefulness. Same in politics. Sorry.

4. Take on the ruling party: Nobody can or has ruled without missteps. Modi is hands-on and enjoys people's trust. Thus, attacking him does go against the public mood at the moment. However, the triumvirate can pick the genuine mistakes, fight the right battles and reclaim some political ground. The BJP government will make mistakes, and the Congress has to spot these opportunities and react to them with grace in a fair and constructive manner. It has to be solution-oriented criticism, not 'they are all crooks' nonsense or glib comebacks.

5. Tell us how things will be different: What has changed in the Congress that, should it come back to power, a CWG or 2G will not, and cannot, happen again? How will we be sure that arrogance won't be tolerated in the party? How are we to be sure that Rahul, and the triumvirate, will make themselves chamcha-proof? Unless these questions are answered with real actions, trust will never be regained.

These steps aren't easy, and require transformation of an old organization that isn't used to losing and changing. Still, for the sake of our democracy, a cleansing is worth the attempt. Time is running out. Change, or perish. Swachh Congress, anyone?

Once upon a Beehive

Once upon a time, there was a giant beehive. It was located in an ancient tree that was situated amidst meadows and gardens filled with bright and colourful flowers.

The beehive had a queen bee, who, along with some senior bees, had been chosen to run the hive. Collectively, the elected were called the government. Worker bees entrusted the government bees with storing their honey and keeping them safe. The government also had to discover new gardens, to provide new sources of flowers and nectar for the new generation of baby bees.

To ensure stability and avoid chaos, the government bees made rules and passed laws. The worker bees had to follow them, else they could be punished. This was particularly important because the beehive had different kinds of bees, who could end up fighting with each other. The black bees and the brown bees were the two main kinds. They essentially did the same work. However, they had slightly different looks and practised their own prayer habits.

In good times, it was the perfect beehive. Over time, however, things changed. Government bees had their own kids, relatives and friends. Most could not join the government. They had to become worker bees like everyone else. However, one day, a senior government bee's son told his father that being a worker bee was too much work. 'Why not let me take a bit of honey from our reserves?' he said.

'But that would be wrong,' the father bee said.

'Nobody would find out. What happens in the government, stays in the government,' replied the government bee's son. He was right. Worker bees trusted the government more than they did themselves. A bit of honey lost would not be noticed at all.

And then it started. Slowly, all government bees' children, cousins, relatives, friends and well-wishers started stealing a bit of honey every day from the reserves. They didn't have to slave in the gardens all day anymore. The worker bees did notice that the honey levels were not going up as expected. When some worker bees pointed this out, the government just ordered everyone 'to work harder and not be lazy'.

The worker bees worked harder to make more honey. However, honey levels refused to rise. In fact, they started to fall.

Soon, government bees started another practice. Whenever they found a new garden, they gave it to their children, friends and relatives first. 'What the worker bees don't know, the worker bees won't miss,' was the hushed conversation in government circles.

Over time, not only did honey levels fall, the discovery of new gardens stopped for the kids of worker bees. They remained idle and hungry. Sometimes, the queen bee tossed some scraps at the worker bees, and everyone praised the queen. However, the scraps were not enough.

'Who is stealing the honey?' an influential worker bee finally asked one day.

The government noticed that the influential protesting bee was black. So the government said, 'The brown bees are doing it.'

Then the government called the brown bees, and told them, 'We think the black bees are stealing all your hard work.'

Hungry and tired, the black and brown bees were filled with anger. They fought with each other. The government bees enjoyed the distraction and continued to steal. As brown and black bees died and suffered, the government tossed some more honey scraps. Worker bees praised the queen again.

Soon, there was a drought. The flowers became few, and it was time to turn to the honey reserved over all these years. However, to everyone's shock, there was no honey in the reserves at all. Worker bees, normally trusting of the government, went to check the government bees' and their relatives' homes. They found everyone fat and sitting on their own private reserves of honey. What's more, they also found maps of hundreds of new gardens that were discovered but never shared with the worker bees.

Dismayed and shocked, the worker bees came back to their poor homes. The brown and black bees looked into each other's eyes. They realized they had been fooled. They hugged each other and apologized for all the hurt they had caused each other.

'We will teach them a lesson,' the black and brown bees said in unison. The worker bees realized that the time had come to use their sting, not against each other, but against those who had cheated them.

Meanwhile, the queen bee sensed the tension. She presented her beautiful young son. 'He will save you now. Like I did all these years.'

However, the brown and black bees were smarter now. They gathered together in a swarm and unleashed their stings on the government and their fat cronies. The government bees barely had any time to collect their belongings. They simply had to run away from the hive. Soon, they were all gone.

The brown and black bees decided to select their best people to be in charge. Also, they decided to never blindly trust, but monitor everyone. The hive recovered, and the new generation worked hard to restore the honey stores. New gardens led to new prosperity, and the beehive became the most successful beehive in the world.

A few years later, an old bee, talking to her grandson at

night, said, 'Did you know we had a queen bee at one time?'

'Yes. But we don't anymore. Because deep down, there's a little king in all of us,' replied the baby bee.

ECONOMY

Rescue the Nation

> If the babus want, they can fix the system much faster than any external activist, artist or media person can.

Our bureaucracy runs our country. Our politicians have little interest in the nuts and bolts of running the country. Politicians like symbolism—meals at Dalit homes, presidential selections and cartoons. Or they like issues that appeal to vote banks—religious quotas, temple locations and dividing up states.

While politicians entertain us, the babus ensure the country doesn't completely shut down. Railway officers ensure that trains run, municipal officers get garbage collected, junior Indian Administrative Service (IAS) officers manage districts and senior IAS officers run entire ministries.

The stereotype of the babu is someone who is lazy, conservative, arrogant and corrupt. For sure, a significant number of babus may justify the typecasting. However, a large number of civil service officers work hard and are honest. Many of my own college batchmates are part of the civil services. They work twelve-hour days, in hostile, demotivating conditions at a tenth of the salary they could earn in the private sector. It is perhaps their madness, a misplaced idealism, a love of the country or a feeling that they are making a difference.

These are smart people. Clearing the civil service exam is no mean feat. These people would be highly valued outside the government. Any foreign multinational setting up in India would do well to hire an ex-IAS officer, if only for his or her ability to work through the Indian system. Civil service professionals are well-educated, intelligent, influential and capable.

And yet, one shortcoming keeps this entire class of people from earning as much glory as it could. And that is—no guts.

Sorry to say, but despite all their qualities, government babus are some of the most scared people on earth. They are scared of their politician bosses, worried about their annual performance appraisals, too attached to their promotions and afraid of lagging behind in their careers. They enjoy job security and periodic raises in their salaries and perquisites even if they do not show extraordinary performance. On the other hand, they can suffer if they stick their necks out, suggest improvements or point fingers at wrongdoers. So they often maintain the status quo. Hence, some of the brightest people in the country, close to the corridors of power, aware of what is right and wrong, do little of what is required.

They are doing their jobs, for sure. However, they are not fighting for change. They are petrified. And that is a shame, not only for the civil service community, but also for the entire nation. The babus should answer some basic questions. What are you so scared of? Missing a promotion? Not becoming a secretary? Losing out on an extra bedroom in the subsidized government accommodation? What is the worst that could happen if you raised your voice against inefficient and corrupt masters? Lose your job and this fake temporary power? Do you have no faith in your talent, that you will be able to make a living outside? After working so hard to clear a merit-based exam, does your conscience not trouble you every time you see your bosses plunder the country?

More than anything, babus need to answer this—what is your dharma? To listen to your masters or to do the right thing?

According to the Mahabharata, Krishna advised Arjuna to fight his own cousins. Since Arjuna was fighting a virtuous war, it became his dharma to fight and not give in to attachment. The babus need to sit down and reflect on their own new dharma.

For if the babus want, they can fix the system much faster than any external activist, artist or media person can. The babus are in the system and know what is going on. The babus are the most powerful lobby in the country. If they agitate, politicians in the corridors of power will have to listen..

Don't sit idle and watch injustice happen. Rebel if you need to. Don't become part of the evil, because you have enough talent to be successful by being good.

Rise, fight and rescue us. The country needs you. Your time has come.

To Make 'Make in India' Happen, Delete Control

> If we really want them to 'Make in India',
> the government has to let go.

India Park. It has swings, nature trails, flower beds, sports facilities and walking tracks. Everything is wonderful, except for one thing: kids don't come to play here. This is because the park is mostly used by senior citizens, whom the kids refer to as 'uncles'. Over a hundred uncles use the park for their morning/evening walks, society meetings and yoga classes. Each uncle also carries a stick, and uses it on the few kids who happen to venture into the park. If a kid jumps too much, squeals in delight, climbs up a tree or plays cricket, the uncles whack the kids. After all, the uncles feel, the park must be kept in order. There is even a microphone system installed that warns kids to behave.

As expected, the kids soon abandon the park. They go across town to China Park, where they are made to feel welcome. There are rules in that park too—the kids are told to keep the place clean and not hurt anyone. But apart from that, they are encouraged to have fun. The only kids who still use India Park are those who have figured out how to manage the uncles. Whenever they come to play, they bring treats for the uncles—a box of sweets, cold drinks or newspapers. The uncles then leave them alone for a bit. However, the number of kids doing this is small, as bribing uncles is not what most good kids do. India Park, hence, is mostly empty and underutilized.

Then the uncles of India Park start wondering why few kids come to play there while twenty times the number go to China Park. The uncles have meetings, sticks kept on their laps, to discuss the solution. They put up huge signs outside the park, saying 'Kids Welcome'. However, nothing seems to change.

In the above story, replace the uncles with the Indian government, kids with foreign direct investors, fun with legitimate profit and India Park with India. This sums up how we approach the global investor community. We want it here, but we want to beat it with a stick and shout at it the moment it starts having some fun (or earns rewards, in terms of legitimate profits).

This is why we have a long way to go to achieve the prime minister's 'Make in India' goal. The hardest part in achieving this is not the manufacturing infrastructure we need to set up; it is the 'control freak' mindset that exists in our corridors of power (or rather, in any Indian entity with power).

So we say we will never use the retrospective tax laws (which effectively allow the government to change tax laws for previous years and take more money), but we don't remove the laws either. The uncles say, 'We will keep the stick, but we will never use it.' Well, maybe not today, but what if another uncle comes tomorrow? Are the rules going to depend on the uncle's personality? We want companies across the world to invest here, but the government places so many controls and requires so many permissions that it effectively controls every business. We call it free-market capitalism, but in reality it is state-controlled capitalism. The only way the uncles will let you do business is if you keep giving them enough treats. This is how India has been run since Independence, and that is why it is difficult to change the mindset. The unfortunate part is that this uncle-and-stick model keeps the park empty. If investors don't come, we don't have jobs or growth. Kids can play in other parks. Asian economies, Eastern Europe and Latin America are all competing for investor dollars and to be manufacturing hubs. The only way the investors will come is if the rules are clear, simple and not politician-personality dependent—in spirit, writing and practice.

If we really want them to 'Make in India', the government has to let go. Keep business rules, but align them with international standards. Get the government out of business, not just in terms of selling public sector enterprises, but also having no arbitrary or discretionary control over individual businesses. All this should be personality-proof. The current finance minister may be investor-friendly. The next one may not. If I have invested money in India, how can I be sure the new guy won't come after me with a stick?

All these issues have to be addressed if we want economic and employment growth which, come to think of it, is what makes 'acche din' happen. Let go of the sticks, uncles; let the kids come and play.

Pro-poor or Pro-poverty?

> We are still one of the poorest nations on earth.

Poverty is a terrible thing. There are few things as demeaning to human beings as not having the means to fulfil their basic needs in life.

India is one of the poverty havens of the world. We have all heard of India's poverty-stricken millions, probably since childhood. While one could blame the British for all our mistakes pre-1947, it has been nearly seventy years since they left. We are still one of the poorest nations on earth. Many countries in Asia that started with similar poverty levels in the 1940s have progressed faster—some of them dramatically. We, however, remain poor.

The continuance of poverty is particularly surprising because there are so many smart and powerful people who claim to be representing the poor. Politicians, academics, development economists, non-governmental organizations (NGOs)—there are so many people trying to help the poor. It is baffling, then, why we can't seem to get rid of poverty. Our public debates are virtually controlled by left-leaning intellectuals, who are some of the most pro-poor people on earth. And yet, they seem to be getting nowhere.

Well, they won't. Because while they may be experts on the poor and their suffering, they have little idea about the one thing that eventually removes poverty—money. Yes, it is over-simplistic, but it is perplexing how little our top thinkers and debate-controllers know about wealth creation, true economic empowerment, productivity and competitiveness. For, if they did, they would not support one of the most hare-brained schemes to have ever come out of our illusionist politicians' hat—the Food Security Bill, which is now the National Food Security Act.

It is a tough act to write against. The fashionably left, almost communist, intellectual mafia will nearly kill you. The subject is sensitive. You may argue that the numbers just don't add up—that we will ruin our already fragile economy further if we do this. The retort will be 'at least a poor mother will see her child sleep peacefully at night on a full stomach'.

Try arguing with that! You may see financial ruin for the nation, but how will your data-filled presentation ever compete with the picture of a hungry, malnourished child in an Indian village? It can't. I submit that all economics, basic arithmetic, common sense, rationality, practicality fails when someone confronts you with 'so basically you don't want to help the poor, right?'

Nobody does not want to help the poor. Nevertheless, after being labelled anti-poor, you will be labelled an MNC-favouring, FDI-obsessed capitalist. Stay long enough; you will be branded right wing, perhaps with a 'communalist' slur added. Welcome to India, where one doesn't debate based on reason but based on emotions, moral one-upmanship and attacking the debater rather than the argument.

Therefore, like any sane, self-preserving individual, I'd say that my official line is that I was always in favour of the act.

In fact, I propose a better alternative. Why just two-thirds of India, let's extend free grain to the entire country. Moreover, why not some vegetables and fruit too? And don't poor kids deserve fresh milk? We should provide that too. If the debate is going to be won by the guy with the noblest intention, then I am going to make sure I am the one.

Every Indian family must get grain, fruit, vegetables, milk and whatever else it takes to have a healthy and balanced diet. It should be free. There, am I not the good guy now?

When irritating questions pop up in my head about who will pay for it, or how will so many commodities be secured, or how will the already debt-ridden government finance this, I will tell my mind to shut up. I'll avoid looking at the astronomical bill (lakhs of crores over a few years). If I feel this money could be used to transform rural education, irrigation or road networks, which would make our poor empowered, employable and richer, I will scold myself for thinking logically.

It is not important to remove poverty. It is only important to come across as a person who cares for poor people. And I do, more than you. That is why my act will have fruit and vegetables. Does yours? So what if our fiscal deficit swells, the rating agencies downgrade us to junk credit and foreign investors stop investing in our country? We don't need them. They are all our enemies anyway.

We won't have money to spend on productive assets, we'll scare the foreigners away and we will never have good infrastructure, schools or hospitals. So what? At least we care for poor people. We'll keep caring for poor people until our money totally runs out, the nation gets bankrupt, inflation is out of control and there are no more jobs.

Of course, that means far more people will be poorer than from where we started. But isn't that a good thing? After all, it gives us a chance to care for even more people. So, bring on my Food, Fruit, Vegetables and Milk Security Act. Did I miss something in that? Oh yes, nuts. We do need nuts. Some nuts for all Indians, please. You know the kind of nuts I am talking about, right?

The Tiny-bang Theory for Setting Off Big-bang Reforms

> Yes, Indians want change but, at the same time, are scared of it. The trick is to come up with creative political and economic solutions that lead to reform and minimize political damage.

One of the most honest statements from a government official in recent times came from chief economic adviser Arvind Subramanian, who said big-bang reforms are not applicable to a country like India. At a recent event, he said, 'If you look around the world, big-bang dramatic reforms happen around crisis.' He also added, 'Big-bang reforms are not easy to happen in democracy. In democracies, you have multiple veto centres, multiple decision-making centres and it is very difficult to push through decisive change, and if you look at India at this juncture, we are not in crisis.'

There you go. All you big-bang change seekers, the party is over even before it started. The government has, in effect, said it doesn't want to rock the boat. Things won't change much and things won't change fast. Doesn't matter if the election campaign promised a bold new government. We saw TV ads that had farmers saying '*acche din aane waale hain*' (good times are about to come). Investors and businesses were promised a dramatic change for the better in a Congress-mukt Bharat. Voters were asked to deliver a decisive mandate if they wanted real change. And they did. They came out in droves and gave a mandate no single party has received in thirty years.

What could stop India now? Nothing really.

And yet, the big changes didn't happen. A soft interim budget, a calibrated full-year budget, a few positive statements on taxation (only to be contradicted by an overzealous tax department) and a stuck Land Acquisition Bill show that the new government is tying itself up in knots. Investors are turning impatient, stocks and the rupee have started to slip, and while no India Inc. CEO will publicly criticize the government, the profuse praise has certainly stopped. The only thing going for the government right now is Rahul Gandhi, who at least at present is struck more by wanderlust than power lust. Any reasonably organized opposition would be able to take on this government, and this just within a year of the historic mandate. Look how easily the anti-farmer labelling has stuck. Or how the Delhi elections were lost. Or how there is little certainty about the Bihar assembly election.

Sometimes the government asks, 'What big-bang reforms do you want us to undertake anyway?' Well, that is pretty clear. They revolve around opening up the economy, building infrastructure and making it easier to do business, all of which create jobs and growth and raise revenues for welfare projects. I think the intention is there. The government has many extraordinarily capable people, fully aware of what it takes to restore high growth—full rupee convertibility, simple taxation, the goods and services tax (GST) law, no hounding of businesses to score political points, broadening the income-tax base, selling non-productive government assets and the like.

So why don't they do it? Because, as the chief economic adviser stated, change isn't easy in a democracy. Though a billion-plus people feel things need to change, everyone has a different idea of what that change is. I might think a more capitalist approach is better. Another citizen may want all big companies to be banned. Some believe every time the government does something business-friendly, it only helps rich people. Others may be of the view that thriving businesses lead to growth, jobs and tax collections.

And since Indians are closet socialists, trusting a more capitalist set-up is proving difficult for our citizens. Abuse can occur both in socialist and capitalist systems, but a capitalist society does tend to get richer. However, Indians would rather have fewer opportunities and be in a familiar, oppressive system than trust a new system. Until that mentality changes, which means until all of us change, there cannot be a big-bang reform. The political risk of shoving change on people who are not ready for it is simply too high. The only time it happened was in 1991, a time of crisis, and that is somehow the only time Indians became one and listened to reason.

If we do want big-bang reform, many tiny-bang changes are required in the mindset of Indians. The rich versus poor, farmers versus corporates, foreign versus desi conflicts that we have created in our heads deny us the belief that win–win situations are possible. All this doesn't mean that the government does nothing. It promised an agenda of growth, and it has to somehow deliver on it. Some political risks will have to be taken for India's good—what else is a bold government anyway?

Yes, Indians want change but, at the same time, are scared of it. The trick is to come up with creative political and economic solutions that lead to reform and minimize political damage. Rupee convertibility, for example, is a less political issue than the land bill, and perhaps that could be taken up first. A few big-bang items, along with proper communication to change mindsets, would do us all good. Giving up, or going too slow, won't. Sometimes, in life or politics, not taking a risk is the biggest risk.

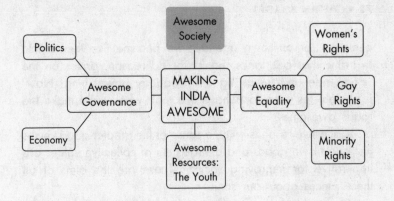

AWESOME SOCIETY: WHO WE ARE AS A PEOPLE AND WHAT WE NEED TO CHANGE

What is a country, really? A piece of land and a group of people who decide to organize themselves. The land is inanimate and fixed. If you want to change the country, it is the people who need to do it. It is the people who can change themselves, and in turn change the country. This change could make it more awesome or make it worse.

We often feel that it is not we but someone else who is at fault for India's problems, usually the authorities. The fact that we, as citizens, refuse to take the responsibility of making India better, is a huge roadblock in making India awesome. We could have the most amazing leaders, the best policies and the strictest laws; however, if we the people don't care about what the leaders do or about following laws, nothing good can happen.

Let us take an example, of traffic in a city. The best traffic cops in the world cannot do anything if the entire traffic decides to not follow the rules. If all we care about is ourselves, or our own agenda, we become like the vehicle in traffic that cuts lanes, honks for no reason, drives on the wrong side and jumps signals if nobody is watching. Now, if all vehicles were to behave like that, who would make the roads awesome?

Collective responsibility, a sense of the greater good versus just one's own good, and a strong set of collective values are imperative for improving society. These are the aims of all these pieces about our society.

In 'Time to Face Our Demons', I have attempted to make people own up to the fact that we are prejudiced and we would rather point fingers than look within. 'We Have Let Them Down' talks about how we don't treat our fellow Indians from the Northeastern states right. 'Watching the Nautch Girls' discusses the draconian ways of the BCCI and how they impact the sport we all love. 'Let's Talk about Sex' and 'The Real Dirty Picture' urge us to confront sexual issues, a taboo in our culture, but extremely important in current times, given the rising rate of crimes against women. 'Saying Cheers in Gujarat' talks about the hypocrisy and senselessness of prohibition in Gujarat, something that is anyway a total failure in implementation. 'Our Fatal Attraction to Food' and 'Junk Food's Siren Appeal' talk about how Indians need to eat right to remain healthy. 'Mangalyaan+Unlucky Tuesdays' talks about the need for us to think in a more scientific way and let go of silly superstitions. In 'India-stupid and India-smart' I discuss some of the irritatingly stupid procedures followed in Indian airports. 'Cleanliness Begins at Home' is a contribution to the government's Swacch Bharat campaign, and talks about how it can actually happen. 'Bhasha Bachao, Roman Hindi Apnao' is a radical thought, talking about the importance of Roman Hindi—Hindi, but in the Roman script—in today's times of Whatsapp messaging and Facebook statuses. Finally, 'A Ray of Hope' celebrates the Jaipur Literature Festival, which is among the best literary festivals in the world. All the issues covered in this section are not only of national importance, but also directly touch an individual.

After all, an awesome society will automatically lead to an awesome nation.

Time to Face Our Demons

> We don't really want to understand what it is about us that we can be so easily incited to burn trains or to riot.

In all my years of writing columns, this has to be the most difficult piece to write. For I'm going to discuss one of the darkest chapters in India's history—the Godhra train carnage and the subsequent riots that took place in February–March 2002. You may wonder why I'm doing so now, after all these years. Why open old wounds that will only cause more pain? Why not just bury the past?

Well, you can bury the past, but you cannot bury wounds. Wounds need to be healed. The event has been covered, discussed and unceasingly analysed in the media and public forums. It has shaped the politics of our country. And yet, I feel we have not done something essential that is required to come to terms with such a tragedy. We haven't faced our demons.

For if you start any debate on the Godhra incident, within minutes it degenerates into these two arguments—(a) the Hindus retaliated because the train carrying Hindus was burnt first; or (b) innocent Muslims were targeted by fundamentalist Hindus, who used the train incident to commit genocide. Both arguments look reasonable enough. However, they do not provide a solution. Inherently, these arguments are about blame. They can be reduced to (a) 'you did it' or (b) 'no, you did it'. Little wonder no closure has been reached in thirteen years.

We have also tried to attach villains to the incident. Blame that guy, he caused it. It is usually the slimy, wily, greedy politician—whom we love to assign as the root cause of all problems in India.

It is amazing how every Indian feels there is a problem in our system and someone else is to blame for it. We need someone we can point fingers at, for misleading us, looting us, dividing us and keeping us backward. It is a comforting narrative, 'I am a good citizen who cares for India. The rest of them are keeping us behind.'

Really? If everyone feels the problem is with the rest, then who is really at fault? Perhaps the problem may actually be with us?

We don't want to face the ugly truth. We don't really want to understand what it is about us that we can be so easily incited to burn trains or to riot. We don't think we are in any way responsible for what happened.

Sure, the reader of this book isn't a criminal and didn't kill anyone. However, ask yourself this. Are we, at some level, guilty of feeling sentiments that are not in the best interest of India? Do a lot of us not, at some level, harbour mistrust for the other religion? In peaceful times, we can talk about unity and peace. However, God forbid, five terror attacks happen in the next few months, perpetrated by criminals who are Muslim. Will Hindus not start doubting Muslims again? Will we not start calling them names, or talk about sending them to Pakistan, or how they are the reason for almost every Indian problem? Will we not develop a public opinion that the Muslims need to be kept in check? And then, in that environment, if there are anti-Muslim riots after an attack, will we not give the perpetrators of those riots some sympathy or validation? If yes, then have we changed at all?

Similarly, if Hindu groups target a few innocent Muslims in

a few stray attacks, will the Muslim community not start to feel vulnerable? If you are a Muslim, will you not feel that Hindus are out to get you? Won't you feel you need special protection, compared to the other Indian citizens? In this scenario, if some politicians come and offer support to your community, will you not back them unconditionally? Will you not pardon all their corruption, inefficiency and lack of accountability, just to feel a little safer?

We are still divided. The attacks on churches in 2015, the Muzaffarnagar riots in 2013 and the riots in Trilokpuri, Delhi, in 2014 prove this. We are still unable to respect India as much as we respect our religion. In peaceful times, this doesn't surface much. However, in volatile times, this brings out the worst in us. The Godhra incident was an example of the worst in us. It was the cost of keeping the country second and religion first. It was the price we paid for thinking religion is so important as to give us the right to break laws or abuse democracy. Unfortunately, the families that suffered in the incident paid the biggest price.

We find reasons to hate each other. We huddle in our groups, not marrying our children to theirs, a clear sign we are divided. We hurt, but we never try to heal. We point fingers, but we never self-reflect. We make little effort to communicate or find common ground, the biggest being that all of us jointly have to take the nation forward.

It isn't just this incident. We have lost a lot as a nation because of these divisions—whether in human life, or bad politics leading to poor development. It is time we stop. It is time we reflect, feel the shame and come to terms with it. There is no one person who needs to apologize for this. We all need to. It is time we face our demons, and tell them we will never allow ourselves to feel the wrong way again. That we will always put the nation first, and not let that resolve be threatened, even in tough times.

If we do this, the healing will begin. We will move ahead as a society that has learnt from the past. We will no longer be swayed.

We cannot compensate for the pain of those who suffered and lost lives. But if we can move on from this as better people, perhaps they will, from the heavens above, forgive us.

We Have Let Them Down

> The rest of India needs to reflect on how our shallow racist thinking has hurt not only the Northeastern people, but also ourselves.

Every time one visits the Northeast, the locals make one resounding request—please help us get attention. Please treat us like Indians and not as outsiders. Why do they feel this way? Why don't we listen to these eight of our twenty-nine states more? Why does this section of fellow Indians feel isolated even in today's digitally connected age?

Events such as the Assam riots in 2012, the panic exodus of Northeasterners from certain cities in 2012, the abysmal coverage of the Assam floods in 2013 and the racist attack on Arunachal Pradesh student, Nido Tania, in Delhi in 2014 makes it clear we have not been listening to them. The region and its people have several issues, but they fail to get mainstream attention. They fester, and we often don't discuss them until it is too late.

Apart from addressing issues, we also need to show empathy and compassion towards the Northeast migrants. The usual route is to be politically correct and say how we are all one and should treat them as our brothers and sisters. Frankly, such sermons don't work. India might be one country. We may be mostly good people at heart. However, we are probably the most internally racist nation on earth. Yes, we all stand up for the national anthem. We also cheer for our cricket team and Olympic medallists. When that ends, however, it's almost like we try to find a reason to hate and mistrust one another. And as part of our shallow thinking, one of the first reasons we discriminate against someone is because they look different from us.

The Northeastern people are beautiful and attractive. They also have slightly different, more Oriental, physical features as compared to the rest of us. So we use it as a reason to ignore, mock or exclude them. It is shameful, disgusting, primitive and sick. Did our schools not teach us to be open-minded, or did our parents reinforce the racism? It is nothing to be proud of. It reflects poorly on us, the discriminators, rather than the Northeasterners. It is also worrisome. For if we cannot accept such superficial differences between our own people, how will we ever engage with the globalized world? Are we going to mock every foreigner who comes to India for business and is not white (towards white people, we are automatically servile)?

Is this the nation we want? Where people look for differences rather than similarities? There is more in common between the Northeastern people and us than we think.

The young people in the Northeast are hungry for a good education and a decent job—much like youth in the rest of India. Northeastern youth also suffer from a lack of good, ethical leaders, poor infrastructure and high inflation. They also see their natural resources being plundered. Like the rest of us, the people of the Northeast pay exorbitant amounts for petrol, an energy price loaded with taxes even as politicians' friends get coal mines for free.

Yes, the Northeastern citizen is one of us. If we all work together, we can put pressure on our leaders to end some of these problems. Or we can continue to fight internally. Just what the politicians want, so they can continue to loot us while we become their vote banks.

The rest of India needs to reflect on how our shallow racist thinking has hurt not only the Northeastern people, but also ourselves. Meanwhile, they could take proactive, practical steps that will put the Northeast back in the reckoning.

Here are five ideas that could work and need further thought:

One, tourism in the Northeast needs to be stepped up. It has some of the most spectacular sights of natural beauty in India. A few more hotel permits, a couple of world-class resorts, some promotion and slightly better connectivity can work wonders there.

Two, lobbying for a low-tax/special economic zone (SEZ)-type city or area can help. India needs a place like that anyway. It will attract investments, jobs and a cosmopolitan culture badly required in the region.

Three, Guwahati to Bangkok is only 2,400 km by road and Imphal to Bangkok is less than 2,000 km. In contrast, Guwahati to Mumbai is 2,800 km away. There are talks of a Thailand–Myanmar–India trilateral highway in the Northeast, and that must be put on top priority. The Northeast can be the gateway to East Asia. It can control a significant portion of India's trade. Once you have business to do, people don't ignore you.

Four, the Northeast can provide incentives, such as land, for the media to move there. Once there is enough media presence, the region will be better covered.

Five, some spectacular events—whether it is the biggest music festival or a carnival—that tie in with the local culture, yet attract the rest of the country, can integrate the region better.

The Northeast has been in the news for the wrong reasons. The rest of us have let down the people there a little. In times to come, let us open our minds to these eight beautiful states. Let us hope that the Northeast finally finds its rightful place, and is no longer an ignored child, but a blue-eyed star of our national family.

Watching the Nautch Girls

> Like a king's nautch girls, our cricket players
> have to do what the BCCI tells them.

The spot-fixing scandal in the Indian Premier League (IPL) 2013 had everything to keep headlines buzzing—money, sex, sleaze, gambling and even a towel visual. Soon, the narrative became about degrading Indian values and the players' greed. Nostalgia experts reminisced about the time when cricket was a gentleman's game. Some blamed the IPL. Others said it was just 'a few rotten eggs'. The typically naïve solution suggested was for the Board of Control for Cricket in India (BCCI) to be stricter, and keep players under control.

It is laughable that the BCCI was charged with the responsibility of keeping players fair. For, it is one of the most talent-exploitative and unfair organizations in the world. Its then president (who is now the chairman of the International Cricket Council [ICC]) N. Srinivasan's son-in-law, Gurunath Meiyappan, was one of those alleged to have a hand in the spot-fixing. The BCCI won't have a solution. It is the problem.

Much has been written about the BCCI's lack of accountability and dishonesty. However, the problem lies in the BCCI's fundamental structure, the power abuse of players it allows and how the IPL is part of that exploitation.

The spot-fixing may have surprised people. However, far more shocking is that we as a cricket-loving nation have allowed our entire cricketing talent to become pawns. Like a king's nautch girls, our cricket players have to do what the BCCI tells them. Else they risk unemployment, banishment and an end to what is an already risky career. The BCCI pays players what it feels like, stops them from joining other leagues and decides the terms of its own league. One can understand an inherent natural monopoly required to create a national team. But how can the BCCI have a monopoly over the IPL? How can it tell players to play the IPL, and nothing but the IPL, when it comes to revenue-generating side activities?

It is important to understand how the BCCI is able to run a sweatshop-like enterprise in full public eye. The BCCI, a private club, through its membership of the ICC, has the mandate to select the national team. This one mandate has allowed the BCCI to exploit every professional Indian cricket player ever born. For, the BCCI will blacklist you from being considered for the national team if you don't dance to its tune. In 2007, a domestic league called the Indian Champions League (ICL) was floated. The BCCI banned players from joining the other league. Why? It wasn't an alternate team to Team India. How on earth did the BCCI get the right to publicly blackmail players into doing what it wants, even when it doesn't affect the national team? Why couldn't our players join domestic league teams wherever they wanted? We, the people, didn't raise questions then. We just sat in the king's durbar and watched the nautch girls' new show.

Soon after, the BCCI copied the ICC's model and launched the IPL. It brought private team owners, but the BCCI decided the revenue sharing between stakeholders and kept control. The IPL had nothing to do with national cricket. And yet, the BCCI could dictate terms to every IPL team owner and player. We, as a nation, did nothing but watched. For, the show was good.

Here are some facts: the BCCI's own website (with very limited, specious disclosure) cites a ₹526 crore overall surplus of income over expenditure for 2013–14. Of this only ₹11 crore was paid to players, a steep dip from ₹49 crore in the previous year because of 'lesser media rights income'.* Is this a fair split? Who decides if it is? If spectators pay for cricket, where would they want the money to go? Of course, add the lack of accountability and control over players, the BCCI also has ample opportunity to milk extra unaccounted-for earnings.

Some may feel that our players are well paid. However, fair payment is not what you decide is reasonable. It is based on the revenue they can generate. Frankly, on that metric, the average player is highly underpaid. Considering the short career span, the competition in reaching professional level and the thousands who try but don't make it—the median player incomes are low as compared to what the game can and does generate. The reason—the BCCI. And when incomes are unfairly low, the mother organization is exploitative and doesn't respect talent, is it a surprise when players choose the wrong way of boosting incomes?

What needs to be done? Well, a structural fix will work best. The BCCI can keep the national team mandate (someone has to). However, the BCCI should be divested of the IPL. The IPL is a separate revenue-generation activity. Let our cricketers have control over it, along with the partners they choose. Domestic leagues have no bearing on the national team, and the BCCI has no reason to exploit players for the same. We as spectators, too, need to realize the urgency and importance of cricket reform. If you care for cricket, help fix it. Raise your voice, share your concern and reach out to your politician against the BCCI's exploitation of your stars. The players will thank you for it. Release Indian sport from the clutches of these mediocre power exploiters. That is the real game right now. Otherwise we will continue to remain spectators watching the nautch girls.

---

*https://relaunch-live.s3.amazonaws.com/cms/documents/ BCCI%20AR%20Media%20Book.pdf

Let's Talk about Sex

> We need to refresh our societal values around sex. Else, the problems and hypocrisy related to sex will never go away.

The title of this piece alone was probably enough to make you close your book and look around to check that no one was watching you read it. Yes, we Indians don't like to talk about sex. It is taboo, against our culture, bad for society, corrupts young minds and distracts people from the right path. In fact, it is perverted, dirty and something to be ashamed of.

With so many pejoratives, it is no surprise that most Indians keep their views about sex private. Else, they fear being branded characterless persons. Women have to be extra careful. A good Indian woman is supposed to be almost asexual, to be considered pure and chaste. Indian culture wants us to be sexual only in the institution of marriage, for purposes of procreation. Any deviation and you are a person of loose morals, harmful to yourself and society.

We weren't always like this. History scholars would agree that our ancient texts, such as the Mahabharata and the Puranas, are quite candid about sex and portray a fairly liberal society. So, what happened? What made India so stuck up?

Many theories exist. Some say centuries of rule by conservative Mughal rulers and the puritanical British made us this way. Others say influential Brahmin priests created draconian rules. Whatever the reason, India today is largely conservative. No politician, for instance, will even discuss sex, let alone express his views or take a stance around a topic of a sexual nature. The default strategy of living in Indian society is to pretend that sex doesn't exist (ignoring how our population got to over 1.2 billion, of course).

Unfortunately, such a strategy doesn't work over time. This is because we are Indians later, humans first. Nature has made sex a powerful internal force. This force is so strong that despite all the progress and comforts designed by humanity, the desire for sex still remains. People, Indians or non-Indians, are interested in sex.

However, since we shun it so much, we have two major problems. One, repressed sexual desire often comes out in unsavoury ways. Two, we are unable to discuss or have a meaningful debate around any topic to do with sex.

Repressed sexual desire, for instance, is manifest in child sexual abuse, which is rampant in India. Apart from this, the many instances of molestation, the feeling of a lack of safety amongst our women, the brutal rape cases are all at least partly due to this repressed desire gone bad.

Another less harmful, but significant and widespread trait due to such repression, is the double lives many Indians lead, especially amongst the youth. People are not open to talking about dating or sex with their families, where they are expected to be falsely pious. As a result, there are lies and avoidable hypocrisy.

The second major problem of our 'let's pretend sex doesn't exist' society is that nothing sexual can be meaningfully discussed. The clumsy handling of the age of consent issue in 2013, shifted from eighteen to sixteen and back to eighteen, is a case in point. The legal age of consent is a complex topic worldwide. It involves several issues such as prevalent practices in society, individual liberties and the potential misuse of existing laws. However, with our prevalent anti-sex attitudes, we view the age of consent as nothing more than a licence or even encouragement to have sex. Anyone arguing for age sixteen, even though it may be better suited from a practical, legal and current societal standpoint, would be seen as encouraging promiscuity. Little wonder the government panicked and withdrew the proposal to reduce it to sixteen.

Similarly, the rape law amendments, while mostly welcome, saw limited debate. Our society doesn't allow debate around such topics. 'Punish them as harshly as possible' is the only guiding principle. There is little discussion on potential abuse of laws, the difficulty in proving charges in many of the cases or what else we could do outside of setting up new laws to prevent sexual crimes against women.

In several ways, India is modern and free compared to other nations. We have free speech, a free media and secularism. We have no laws forcing us to practise any religion or dress in a particular manner. Recent advances in technology have meant that people are also connected like never before. This means that our youth, brought up in this modern environment and curious about sex, like their counterparts around the world, will be unable to follow our traditionally strict anti-sex attitudes.

This does not mean we should open the floodgates and make it an 'anything-goes' society. However, we need to refresh our societal values around sex. The traditional versus modern balance needs to shift a little towards the modern, and be more suited to current times. Else, the problems and hypocrisy related to sex will never go away.

Where do we want India to be in terms of sexual attitudes today? I don't want to propose or impose an answer. It will come only if we discuss the issue in an open and inclusive manner—between rich and poor, young and old, feminists and others. Only then can we find solutions to the problems around sex that India faces today.

So take a deep breath and say, 'We are Indians. And yes, sometimes we can and need to talk about sex.'

The Real Dirty Picture

> By shunning pleasure we are simply turning ourselves into a society of liars and hypocrites.

Few things bring out Indian hypocrisy more than any reference to sex. We blush, pretend it doesn't exist, look the other way, change the topic, hate the person who brought it up and do whatever we can to avoid confronting a healthy, balanced discussion on it.

In fact, many say sex is against Indian culture, a bizarre notion for a country that reproduces faster than most others. Perhaps what the culture-protectors are saying is that sex for pleasure is bad. And since Indian culture does nothing bad, sex is against Indian culture. Hence, politicians maintain a public stance about women covering up and pre-marital sex being immoral, and censor anything remotely sexy.

And yet, I can bet a number of politicians and babus watch porn. Remember the incident in Karnataka in 2012, when some ministers were caught watching porn in the state legislative assembly? In fact, most people who have access to porn watch porn. While only a few have the daredevil spirit and stupidity to watch it in a legislature, they all consume this product that is super deadly to Indian culture. In fact, a significant number of women watch porn too, though they may not get as excited about it as say, a 50 per cent sale on their favourite handbag.

So why are we like this? Why are we so two-faced about something so natural? It is a difficult question to answer, but we weren't always this way. Our ancient texts, such as the Upanishads, discuss sex in an explicit manner. The Mahabharata refers to Draupadi's polyandry. The temples in Khajuraho leave little to the imagination.

Perhaps our attitudes changed during centuries of Mughal and Victorian rule, both not exactly known for their liberal attitudes. Add a bit of Brahminical puritanism to it and somewhere down the line, Indians began to frown upon all pleasures, particularly sex.

Hence, we have heavy taxes on alcohol. And of course, states like Gujarat have banned alcohol. Movie tickets carry an entertainment tax, quite unjustified as people buy them with their already taxed income anyway. I am quite sure that if the government could, it would tax sex.

However, none of these prohibitions and taxes works. People drink anyway, even if they have to consume cheaper-quality, more harmful stuff. Alcohol is easy to source in Gujarat, and has led to a massive illegal bootlegging industry. People who cannot afford movie tickets watch pirated movies, thus hurting the film industry.

The simple fact that governments and culture-keepers don't realize is this—you cannot stop people from doing what they enjoy. In a country like India where enforcement of law is weak, this is even more applicable. By shunning pleasure, we are not preventing people from experiencing it. We are simply turning ourselves into a society of liars and hypocrites.

And that is the important question. What is worse? Watching porn or being dishonest?

Our pornography laws (enacted in 1969, surely no pun intended) are archaic. Can we make them more practical, so we do not force millions of Indians into lying every day? And similarly, we need to stop looking at pleasure and enjoyment as sin. Human life is limited, and if we don't enjoy our time here, what is the point of it? Yes, excess of anything, from sugar to alcohol to porn, can be harmful. Exploitation is also bad. However, it doesn't mean you classify moderate consumption as immoral, or against the national culture.

It is time to reform our moral standards. Let people have fun in moderation. Let us accept human behaviour, rather than make the nation live a lie. We work hard when we have to, but sometimes we can enjoy a drink. It doesn't make us good or bad people. It just makes us who we are. And it is time Indians became comfortable with themselves.

Saying Cheers in Gujarat

> When hundreds of millions of people around the world can handle a few drinks...why does the state have to impose laws curtailing consumption in a particular region?

As I've said earlier, we Indians are masters at avoiding uncomfortable topics. We would rather be hypocrites and liars than discuss something uncomfortable. Besides sex, another topic we have learnt to avoid is consumption of alcohol. In public, we condemn anything to do with alcohol. In private, millions of Indians enjoy their drinks. This includes not only businessmen and corporate types, but also politicians, doctors, teachers and journalists.

One of the casualties of this hypocrisy is that prohibition laws in certain parts of India are never discussed. Places where liquor is still banned are Mizoram, Manipur, Nagaland, Lakshwadeep and the modern, vibrant Gujarat. Kerala, too, is phasing out alcohol, and aims to become a dry state by 2024. That Gujarat has such a policy is particularly baffling, especially since the state projects itself as one of India's most advanced.

The reasons cited to keep the 1960 prohibition law in place remain the same. The abuse of alcohol, particularly amongst the less affluent, can destroy households. Prevention of crimes against women is a reason to justify the ban. Alcohol-related health problems and the potential for addiction are well known. With so many noble reasons for a ban, one almost wonders why we don't have it in other states too.

However, virtuous intentions aside, there is another side to it. That is, the ban doesn't work. In fact, the extent to which this ban is defied is ridiculous. Alcohol, though bootlegged, is easily available in Gujarat. I have attended various events in the state where surreptitious bar counters were arranged for the party afterwards, complete with bartenders and cocktail mixes. High-profile citizens of the city enjoy their evening tipple and discuss life and work. However, instantly, these respectable people also turn into law-breaking criminals. This happens because of an outdated law which doesn't even apply to over 90 per cent of India's population. When we are encouraging our citizens to break one law, how will they ever respect the other laws? Will it not eventually lead to an 'anything goes' society, which seems to be a big reason for India's problems today?

When hundreds of millions of people around the world can handle a few drinks and run organizations, companies or even countries the next day, why does the state have to impose laws curtailing consumption in a particular region? Excessive fat and sugar consumption is leading to many diseases, some even life-threatening, around the country, Gujarat included. Why not control those substances too? Why are cigarattes and tobacco-laced paans available at every street corner in Gujarat? What's the point of a ban that doesn't work anyway? Will we ever ask these questions or just keep harping on a modern Gujarat but never change what needs to be changed there?

Controlling consumption, of a substance that is legal and is consumed by millions around the world, is not what a modern state would do.

There are many direct losses due to this law. The state loses thousands of crores of excise duty which, in turn, has to be recovered by making other goods and services more expensive. Gujarat is trying hard to promote itself as a global investment destination and a tourist hub. For both these industries, the ban on alcohol has an adverse effect. Indians are okay with the hypocrisy of routinely breaking the law; many foreigners are not. Foreign tourists do not find it exciting or normal to have bootlegged alcohol. Gujarat's beach destinations, for instance, will never thrive unless the alcohol policy is lifted. Tourism creates jobs. With this law in place, we are curtailing employment for thousands of Gujarat's youth.

Similarly, even as an investment destination, this policy is harming Gujarat. There is no global finance city—whether London, New York, Hong Kong, Tokyo, Singapore, Shanghai, Seoul or Mumbai—where alcohol is banned. Global bankers do not want to live in a place where they are doing something illegal every time they attend a party. If Gujarat is serious about becoming a world-class business destination, it needs to benchmark its laws to world-class locations.

Notably, even the United States experimented with prohibition from 1920 to 1933. The reasons cited were the same as in present-day Gujarat. However, the ill effects were the same too. As a result, the laws were repealed. This is what John Rockefeller, initially a supporter of prohibition, had to say in the end:

> When prohibition was introduced, I hoped that it would be widely supported by public opinion and the day would soon come when the evil effects of alcohol would be recognized. I have slowly and reluctantly come to believe that this has not been the result. Instead, drinking has generally increased; a vast army of lawbreakers has appeared; many of our best citizens have openly ignored prohibition; respect for the law has been greatly lessened; and crime has increased to a level never seen before.

Many would agree the above applies to Gujarat too. We must openly debate this issue and reach a conclusion that is practical and helps in the country's progress. I do not endorse drinking. Neither do I consume much alcohol. I do, however, endorse freedom, change and modernity. And that is exactly what Gujarat needs.

Our Fatal Attraction to Food

> We need to be more self-aware of what we eat.

Middle-class Indians have a passionate relationship with their food. It is one of the few forms of pleasure our society readily accepts. We hate alcohol and we pretend sex doesn't exist. We even tax our entertainment. However, when it comes to food, we like to stuff ourselves and everybody else around us. Our weddings have lavish spreads that would make the Victorian royalty blush. Hospitality is measured in terms of one main criterion—how well fed are the guests when they leave.

So one can imagine the outrage when that one, single form of allowable sensual joy is attacked. In May 2015, news reports emerged that the Uttar Pradesh Food Safety and Drug Administration (FDA) had found high levels of monosodium glutamate (MSG) and lead in packets of Maggi noodles, the staple snack and even meal for many Indian households.* Both these substances are harmful to health when consumed in large quantities. Post the report, many people started hoarding packets of Maggi, fearing it would go off the shelves!

This reminds me of a study released by the Centre for Science and Environment (CSE) in 2012, referring to harmful substances in some of the yummiest snacks brought into India

*http://indianexpress.com/article/india/india-others/post-recall-up-fda-tests-more-batches-of-maggi/

by our caring MNCs. A huge reaction ensued. Over tea and bhujias, cold drinks and samosas, butter chicken and naan, Indians held discussions on how what they considered the love of their life—delicious yummy food—could be harming them. The CSE study hit where it hurt most—instant noodles, potato chips and cold drinks are all middle-class indulgences. In scientific mumbo-jumbo, like trans-fat content and percentage daily intake, terms few understand, it said something like, 'This stuff is bad for you.'

The MNCs jumped, engaging public-relations firms to clarify that they had been misunderstood. After all, anybody advertising their products with cute baby voices or other emotional tugs, like grandparent-hugging, could hardly be making anything harmful. If you believe the ads, chips and colas make you a more loving, endearing person and burgers and fried chicken help you make better friends.

So what is going on? Are they really that bad? Don't people eat chips and lead long, healthy lives? And what on earth is this trans-fat and non-trans-fat business? Well, while there is no need to hyperventilate, there is reason for concern.

The modern Indian middle-class diet is turning from bad to horrible. As they get a whiff of affluence, Indians see more money as an excuse to ingest more calories. We are already culturally trained to love food. Easy availability of tasty but unhealthy food has made it worse. Add lack of awareness among the masses and manipulative advertising, and the situation could turn horrible.

The CSE and FDA reports aside, one doesn't need a laboratory study to figure out that some of the things we eat are bad for us. Here are some simple facts. A juice brand sells mango nectar that can have eight spoons of sugar per glass. A pack of instant noodles is nothing but unrefined processed starch (plus MSG and lead, it seems). The malt-based so-called nutritional milk additives for children are mostly sugar. Expensive breakfast cereals can't beat the health value inherent in a few simple rotis. Fried potato chips and burgers with patties that were frozen months ago are quite obviously not healthy.

It isn't just the MNCs. The mithais and namkeens that are part of our traditional heritage, the thick gravies served in Indian restaurants and some homes, and the samosas and pakodas we regularly see being sold at railway stations are equally bad for us. Simple, healthy meals with low oil and sugar are the best. And yet, no one—the government, the MNCs or people like us—seems to care. We shall pay the price in the next ten years. Obesity levels will increase, fitness will decline and healthcare costs will rise. The affluence we feel so proud of will actually come back to bite us.

We need to rein in the MNCs, for they seem to have little ethics. When they are selling something that is harmful in the long term, they should disclose that to the buyer. Children and teenagers should be protected from the onslaught of unscrupulous MNCs that sell junk as aspirational. We need stringent labelling and advertising regulations.

We should laud the studies, which are wake-up calls for all of us. We also need to adopt healthy eating habits in the family. Social engagements should not revolve around food. People need to stop forcing others to eat in order to prove their love. If you love them, let them be healthy.

Taste is an important sense, do not let it lead you to doom. We need to be more self-aware of what we eat. What goes inside us is what finally makes us.

Anyway, all this food talk has made me hungry. How about you?

Cleanliness Begins at Home

> It should not just be 'my home should be clean', but 'my home and the surrounding 10 metres should be clean'.

One of the first signs of a well-managed place, whether it is a restaurant, hotel, airport, office or train station, is its level of cleanliness. If the place isn't clean, it is unlikely to impress anyone. The same applies to an entire country. Indians who travel abroad are often awestruck by cleanliness levels in the developed world.

Therefore, if we want our country to realize its full potential in the world, we have to make it clean. A land of filth, no matter how talented its people and how wonderful its natural resources, will never earn the respect it deserves.

Perhaps this is a reason why the prime minister has taken on the Swachh Bharat mission with such gusto. Not only he but several other influencers and prominent people have lent a hand to the cause, often holding a broom along with it.

However, while the broom in hand does make for a compelling photo-op and is well intentioned, it will take a lot more to clean India. If we are really serious about this, let us first figure out why we are dirty in the first place, and what it would take to have a cleaner India.

We are not dirty people. Indians keep their homes scrupulously clean. In many parts of India, people do not wear shoes inside the house to keep the interiors clean. Some of our religious places are kept clean (though there are exceptions; don't even get me started on Varanasi and Mathura). Diwali, our biggest festival, is the time for spring cleaning. Indians are meticulous about taking a shower daily, which may not be as common in the West.

So why is our country dirty? Why is it that when we step out of our homes, we find the roadside littered? Is it the municipal corporation that isn't doing its job? Is it the local politician who should ensure things are kept clean? Do we not have enough dustbins?

None of this fully explains why India is unclean. The reason is that *we* make it dirty in the first place. And if we truly want to be a clean country, we need to take steps to ensure we minimize filth in the first place, rather than hope someone will pick up a broom and clean it. Developed countries in Western Europe and North America do not have local authorities sweeping the streets all the time. They have systems in place, and the local population cooperates to not create filth in the first place.

We, on the other hand, look at our country differently from our homes. Inside our houses, we want things to be spick and span. Outside the entrance door, it doesn't matter. It isn't mine. It's dirty anyway and how does it matter if I dump some more litter on the streets?

With this mentality—you can have an army of municipal corporation workers working 24×7, a hundred celebrities sweeping the streets, the PM making a dozen speeches—I assure you, India will not become clean.

The only way it can, and will, become clean is if we minimize and prevent the creation of filth in the first place, and the only way that will happen is when all of us together think, 'What is outside my home is also mine.'

This sense of community, recognition of a greater good and collective ownership is the only way for the situation to change. Else, we risk this cleanliness drive becoming another social fad that will be forgotten when the novelty wears off.

Of course, infrastructural improvements, such as new treatment plants for solid, sewage, industrial and agricultural waste, are required. New sets of indices, whether they be measures of cleanliness or density of dustbin distribution, too are needed. Laws and fines have their place as well. All that is indeed the government's job and it will be judged on it.

However, all this will come to naught if we Indians don't change our mentality about what is my space and what isn't. The country is yours. You obviously can't clean all of it, but you can be aware of at least a little bit of area around you. If every Indian has a concept of 'my 10 metres', or a sense of ownership about a 10-metre radius around him or her, magic can happen. Ten metres is just 30 feet around you. Given the number of people we have, we can achieve a lot if we all get together. So it should not just be 'my home should be clean', but 'my home and the surrounding 10 metres should be clean'.

Whenever there is a collective sense of ownership, we have higher cleanliness levels. It is for this reason that most college campuses are cleaner than the city outside, despite housing thousands of youngsters inside.

So get out there, scan your 10 metres. Can you improve anything? A swachh Bharat is indeed possible. The first step is 'swachh manasikta' or clean mindsets. Are you game?

(*In the interests of full disclosure, Prakash Javadekar, Union Minister for Information and Broadcasting as well as for Environment and Forests, nominated me to help with the Swachh Bharat campaign. This piece is one of my contributions towards the campaign. Opinions expressed, however, are independent and personal.*)

India-stupid and India-smart

With some common sense, we can get rid of outdated practices at airports.

You will find many articles on how corrupt and inefficient we are as a nation, particularly our government. However, little is said about something that we all face, but find difficult to admit—the great Indian stupidity. Sure, we have some of the smartest people on earth. World chess champions, software geeks and Fabindia-wearing intellectuals...we have them all. We probably have too many smart people in our country. But allow me, with my moderate intellect, to make one more assertion—we also have a lot of stupid people.

Many of these stupid people are in high places and positions of power, taking stupid decisions for us that make our lives difficult on a daily basis. I cannot cover them all, but let me focus on one particular Indian stupidity hotspot—our airports. Here, one gets to see India's idiocy in full view. Even India's who's who pass through our airports every day and suffer the impact of extraordinary foolish decisions. However, they can do nothing about it.

Here are the top four stupid procedures at our airports:

- One, an absolutely redundant item, is the silly bits of paper with an elastic attached, called hand baggage tags. Passengers attach them to their bags, and they are stamped after passing through the x-ray machine. Later, half a dozen people check your stamp until you board your flight. The stamp and the tag are redundant. Nobody should be able to get bags inside without an x-ray in the first place. If they can, and thus have sneaked in a non-x-rayed, unstamped bag, can't they hide it in another bigger empty stamped bag? While the x-ray is required, the tag-stamp routine is unnecessary. In fact, the stamp creates a false sense of security—it seems like an approval.

- The second stupid routine is during the flight. Most airlines no longer serve free food. They run a snack shop in the aisles mid-flight. The cabin crew takes individual orders, fulfils them, fumbles for change and moves up and down half a dozen times for people who want to use the restroom. It takes the airhostesses forever to inch the cart ahead along the rows. Can't the airlines take food orders during check-in? If they did, the cash would be handled on the ground. Food could be placed on passengers' seats as they entered the aircraft or right after take-off. Wouldn't that be more efficient? Although some airlines now allow you to pre-book meals, why not do the same for snack items and merchandise?

- The third drama occurs when we are about to land. Oftentimes, air traffic control does not give permission to touch down, in case of congestion. Thus, hundreds of aircraft literally burn fuel every day, and delay thousands of passengers. The congestion at some airports has been chronic for many years. Often, the solution is just another runway. Sure, airport runways are sophisticated to make, but aren't they just a nice flat, long strip of road? Why is it so hard to make another runway? Isn't it stupid to waste so much precious fuel (and people's time) every day?

- Stupid situation number four is thrust on passengers arriving in India from abroad. After a long immigration queue to obtain a passport stamp, you queue up again as another official inspects the stamp. How stupid is that? You also write little slips of paper with a customs declaration, which is collected by a sleepy constable as you exit. Nobody ever looks at those slips. The constable often forgets to take them. What is the point of this? Has no one ever questioned this absolute stupidity?

I could go on. The prepaid taxi lines, for instance, where both the tired passengers and the taxi drivers wait for hours because some harried employees fill registers with carbon paper (yes, they still use it!) and cause huge bottlenecks.

While airports are particularly good places to hunt for Indian stupidity, many other Indian processes are retarded too. For example, prepaid SIM forms and the proofs required for them are a joke. They are also easily faked. Places like Dubai, Bangkok or Hong Kong sell working SIMs off the shelf anyway. What are we counting on? For our terrorists to have an aversion to faking Xerox copies, or to have no international friends? Can we let go of this nonsense?

Sure, the issues I mention are not the biggest problems of our country. But they trouble, niggle, irritate and can be easily fixed. Also, if our nation doesn't come across as having a basic level of common sense, it leaves a terrible impression on outsiders. It is also plain dangerous to live with outdated processes. Safety procedures are often inconvenient. However, everything inconvenient doesn't make us safe. It can just be stupid.

Yes, we may be able to live with stupidity, but that is no reason to continue with it. Whoever is in charge of the above or any other stupid procedures, please take steps to change them. Use your brains. Stop behaving like sheep, moving along in silence for decades. We have had enough of India-stupid. It is time we had some India-smart. For now, rubber-stamp this article to show that you have read it.

Bhasha Bachao,
Roman Hindi Apnao

> In the globalizing times we live in now,
> it will do Hindi a lot of good if it also
> welcomes a global script.

One of the perpetual debates in our society is the importance of Hindi versus English. At a broader level, it can be extended to any vernacular language-versus-English debate, and how we risk losing our local languages to English. It is a politically charged issue, with each government trying to show greater allegiance to Hindi than the other.

Consequently, you have the 'promote Hindi' drives, with government offices mandatorily issuing all circulars in Hindi and state-run schools largely being Hindi-medium.

Meanwhile, English continues to grow like never before, without any promotional drive. This is because it offers better career prospects, greater respectability in society, a completely new world of information entertainment and access to technology. After all, you can't even use a mobile phone or basic messaging apps today without a cursory understanding of English.

Understandably, Hindi lovers and purists lament the new society where the youth shun their mother tongue and want to enter the English world as fast as possible. The more they impose Hindi, the more the youth rebel against it.

What is a Hindi lover (myself included) to do?

And what can we all do to save Hindi without making it seem like a burden or obligation?

There is a solution. It is embracing Roman Hindi. Roman Hindi is not Hinglish. It is Hindi language written in the Roman script instead of Devanagari. For example, '*Aap kaise hain?*' is Hindi for 'How are you?', but written in the English script.

Why is this important? Well, because the Roman script is ubiquitous. It is on computer keyboards and telephone touchscreens. It is already popular, especially among the youth. Millions of Indians, for instance, use Whatsapp, where most conversations are in Hindi, although using the Roman script. Sure, Devanagari downloads are available, but few use them. In fact, many Devanagari keyboards on phones use something known as transliteration, where you type in Roman Hindi first and the software will convert the text to Hindi. In other words, the user is still using Roman Hindi.

Roman Hindi is already prevalent in Bollywood posters and in our advertising. Most Hindi movie screenplays are today written in Roman Hindi. Drive around any major city and you are bound to see a hoarding with a Hindi caption written in the Roman script.

However, Hindi experts, purists and defenders are either largely unaware of or indifferent to these developments. They do not see the difference between the Hindi language and its script. People still love Hindi, they just find it difficult to incorporate the script in their modern, technology-driven lives.

We can save Hindi by legitimizing the Roman Hindi script. This will also have a unifying effect on the nation, as it will bring English and Hindi speakers closer. It will also allow other regional languages to become more linked to each other and to English, by virtue of a common script.

Europe, for instance, has more than a dozen different

languages. They share the same script. In Indonesia and Malaysia, the local scripts are long gone and they have adopted the Roman script for their language.

Sure, Hindi purists may not want it this way. They want Hindi to be preserved exactly as it was, with the Devanagari script. However, they forget that languages evolve with the times. And in the globalizing times we live in now, it will do Hindi a lot of good if it also welcomes a global script. In fact, if we make our script globally accessible, it may encourage more people around the world to learn Hindi.

In the past, many Urdu poets published their poems in Devanagari instead of Urdu, only to gain wider acceptance. That was then, but today the need of the hour is to update Hindi to a new version.

We could start with some government notices and public signages in Roman Hindi, and evaluate the response. There is also an opportunity here, as Roman Hindi can create a new print media and books industry. Millions are already using it. It is just that nobody has tapped into the prospects.

Legitimizing a new globally accessible script for Hindi that will be a class leveller can only be good for the language, which otherwise risks being sidelined by the onslaught of English. Let's not see a language from a purist's perspective, but rather as something dynamic and evolving to fit in with the times. *Waqt ke saath badalna zaroori hai*. You understood that sentence, right?

Mangalyaan + Unlucky Tuesdays

> Let there be God in our hearts.
> But let there also be science in our minds.

Few Indian achievements have led to instant national pride as much as the success of the Indian Space Research Organization's (ISRO) Mangalyaan or Mars Orbiter Mission (MOM) to Mars in September 2014. The media gushed, Twitter and Facebook celebrated while every politician and celebrity congratulated ISRO for days. The last comparable Indian gush was the cricket World Cup victory in 2011.

Make no mistake, to place a satellite in Mars's orbit in the first attempt is no small feat. That it was done on a ₹450 crore budget, the cheapest Mars mission so far, makes it even more remarkable. The zeal of the ISRO staff, along with cutting-edge science, made the mission successful. India's pride at MOM's success is justified. However, even as the media machine moves us to other topics, it is worth asking—has MOM made us Indians appreciate and respect science a bit more?

Indians have a schizophrenic relationship with science. On the one hand, we want our kids to take up science subjects in school. Exams to get into top engineering and medical colleges in India are among the toughest in the world. Our students get top scores in science and mathematics, pushing cut-offs higher and higher. If some alien from, say, Mars were to see this, he would think that India is a land obsessed with science. And yet, in many ways, we are completely unscientific.

More superstitions exist in our country than in any other. I am sure many of you have been fed curd and sugar right before a science exam, as a sign of luck. As if some audit department of God above is noting the kids who ate it and hence marking them as deserving of a simpler exam! Babas, astrologers, horoscopes abound. Temple visits are associated with guilt, and often include some sort of a transaction. Place some money in front of the idol and in return some luck will come your way, implying that that is how God thinks about us.

Religious ceremonies spill out on the road, leaving behind a trail of filth and noise pollution. As if that is what God above wants—make the city filthy, bother others, cause traffic jams, make parents reach home to their kids later and then I will be touched by your love.

We also have gods for rain. If a crop suffers due to lack of rain, it is obviously an act of the rain gods. It is not the fault of the irrigation department, which may have had decades of funding but couldn't stabilize irrigation in the area. If there are floods in any state it is God's wrath, and doesn't have anything to do with poor environmental planning and unchecked construction.

If I believe in one God and somebody else in another, the other person is separate from me. If people who believe in my God die, it is more terrible than if people who believe in the other God do.

I don't want to go on and on. All I am trying to say is, do we take the greater message from the ISRO mission? Do we change anything about ourselves?

When sick, we pop pills developed over decades by scientists. We use phones made by scientists to communicate. I type this on a computer made by scientists, and you read this on a screen or paper made with technology. And yet, would you say we Indians have a scientific temperament?

The answer is no, we don't. We want our kids to study

science because it enables them to gain professional degrees that will help them get a job. We want to use science for our selfish interests, but want the option to reject it when it doesn't suit our purposes. For example, gay rights have a scientific basis. However, we don't like those findings and so we bring all sorts of other arguments against them.

If you broaden the definition of science to logical thinking, we fail even more. Almost any argument of tradition, morality, culture and even misplaced patriotism is considered superior to science, if the latter rocks the boat.

Still, we want to celebrate ISRO and MOM. Well, if we really do want to congratulate ISRO, the best contribution we can make is to give science a little more respect in our lives. At its core, science involves logical thinking and a questioning attitude, until a logical and rational solution is arrived at.

We do not have to shun religion. Religion and science are in conflict sometimes. However, given how deeply religious we are, it is unlikely that we can switch over to becoming a purely scientific nation. We have to make both coexist. And in most cases, making science and religion coexist simply involves having a sense of faith to guide you on the path of positivity and goodness, while at the same time using common sense and reasoning to do what is best for you and society.

If India wants to belong to the modern world—which I think we do, given the delirious joy we feel when the developed world acknowledges us—we have to become more scientific. Let the successful mission to Mars be a turning point in the way we look at our world. Let there be God in our hearts. But let there also be science in our minds.

A Ray of Hope

> Let us rejoice that India, once known as the land of scholars and knowledge, still has the best literary festival in the world.

It is a joy to write the rare positive column about something beautiful that takes place in India. The Jaipur Literature Festival (JLF) attracts enormous crowds each time it is held. It put India on the global map.

The JLF's rapid growth is astounding. In 2008, the festival had 2,500 attendees. In 2012, more than 75,000 people participated, a thirty-fold growth in four years. Festival venue Diggi Palace, a family-owned haveli-heritage hotel, burst at the seams on festival days. The eighth edition in 2015, when the festival went beyond Diggi Palace for the first time, with sessions in Amer Fort and Hawa Mahal, saw a record 245,000 footfalls over five days. However, the festival still remains free and open to all. School students, Nobel Prize winners, socialites, scholars, tourists—all enter the gates together to be a part of hundred-plus sessions over five days. The infectious energy of the organizers—Namita Gokhale, William Dalrymple, Sanjoy Roy and Sheuli Sethi—is what makes the festival a success. They work relentlessly every year to run a show that Sanjoy agrees is akin to 'marrying a hundred daughters off at the same time'.

Interestingly, the JLF has given India far better PR worldwide than, say, another initiative of the erstwhile Congress government to do the same—the Commonwealth Games. Unfortunately, most of the Games's news coverage was related to the scam that took place or the shoddiness of the work.

It would be foolish if we did not draw lessons from what makes the JLF such a huge phenomenon:

One, the inclusion of the world's most prominent authors. While not every attending author is a Booker or Pulitzer winner, the JLF has always had a few of them. This gives it enormous credibility and attracts the media. If your event is not truly world class, you will get a fraction of the attention you would otherwise. The Commonwealth Games is no Olympics, and hence the world cares little about it. Be the best, or nobody cares.

Two, the JLF's range of sessions makes it relevant for a wide variety of audiences. International guests can find at least one author they have read or heard about, making them connect to the festival. Readers of popular fiction would find popular authors, not making them feel out of place.

Three, Jaipur is simply beautiful. The architecture is unique and the city is clean and well kept. The government is tourist-friendly. The wonderful Rajasthani people give genuine smiles to strangers. This setting enhances the experience of the visitor, who hankers to come back.

Four, there is a certain humility in the organizers' approach. Despite the literary community being ridden with elitism and snootiness, the JLF manages to keep it classy without being snobbish. There are stories of school students arriving in trains and staying overnight at the platform to attend the festival. For the so-called arbiters of good literature, it must be tempting to sneer at such audiences, but the JLF team has kept away from that attitude.

Five, the festival provides oodles of media-friendly content. Writers have interesting things to talk about and can generate lots of stories for newspapers and TV channels. Naturally, the content-hungry media likes to be there.

Six, the execution is near flawless. As a speaker this year and in previous editions, I have found the logistics perfect; almost all sessions started on time. Execution isn't easy in India, but the JLF gets it right.

At the same time, like all things successful, the JLF has to guard against forces that will try to either exploit its fame or bring it down out of sheer envy. It also has to manage its growth, which seems unstoppable at this point. Here are two suggestions:

One, do not indulge extreme voices beyond a point. Writers like to give their points of view and feel passionately about them. However, the JLF is no activist forum. Too much has already been said about the Salman Rushdie controversy that took place in 2012, but the simple lesson is a zero-tolerance policy at the venue for people who hijack the festival's agenda. The festival has to remain neutral towards all views. It is not a Ramlila Ground.

Also, the festival has to respect local government guidelines, and that includes their security risk perceptions. Even if some esteemed guests oppose or mistrust government policies, the venue is not the place to protest. They can express themselves, but need not take on the government from the venue. They are free to hire a separate protest venue to do it.

Two, the festival will need to consolidate. Modestly priced ticketing won't make the festival undemocratic. There can be flexibility—free days or ticketed days, separate student pricing, donor events, etc.

As a writer, and as an Indian citizen, I feel immensely proud of this celebration of books. Those who say India is all about Bollywood and cricket should pay a visit to the JLF. Silly controversies come and go. Let us rejoice that India, once known as the land of scholars and knowledge, still has the best literary festival in the world.

Junk Food's Siren Appeal

> Following the Maggi ban, it's time to move to a simple label for classifying foods.

Enough has been written about the Maggi controversy, where government labs found more than permissible lead and MSG in packets of Maggi noodles. The resultant PR disaster, confusion and a nationwide recall of one of the most popular products in the country is likely to become a case study in business schools.

However, there is something else as important as the controversy about harmful substances. It is that Maggi noodles, or for that matter any instant noodles, are intrinsically unhealthy, with or without lead and MSG. It is time we have a new, simplified classification system and scale for junk versus healthy food.

Eating refined starch that is processed, dried and kept for months with the help of chemical preservatives is unlikely to be good for you. The ads may be extremely moving emotionally, the brand ambassador could be highly credible and the soupy noodles might taste really good. It is still not good for you.

Hence, even with no MSG or lead, Maggi's tagline of 'Taste Bhi, Health Bhi', seems only half correct. Any nutritional expert will tell you that eating instant noodles for health is about as funny and implausible as using a cheap deodorant to attract dozens of women.

Of course, the noodles won't kill you. Our diet today consists of plenty of other unhealthy foods too. For instance, almost all Indian mithais are unhealthy. As are many of our gravy 'delicacies'. We give up health benefits of food in favour of cost, convenience or taste.

Such compromises are acceptable to an extent. However, in excess they can lead to major health problems such as obesity, heart disease and diabetes.

How does one limit unhealthy food then? The problem comes when junk is marketed as healthy. Our advertising standards for food are extraordinarily lax. Junk-food manufacturers not only hide the nature of their food, but also position them as health-filled alternatives. Armed with ads of beaming mothers feeding sparkly kids, we have junk marketed as emotional nectar every day.

In other sectors such nonsensical advertising would never be allowed. In financial services, there have to be a ton of disclaimers reminding investors of the market risk they take. In cigarettes, we have pictures of blackened lungs on the packs. But packets of potato chips don't bear the picture of an obese heart patient, right?

Food—be it for nourishment or pleasure—has positive associations for us. Any food is good and the kind of food doesn't seem to matter. Perhaps this comes from a time when India was poorer and food was scarce. When we worked twelve hours a day in the fields and could eat and burn as many calories as we wanted. This was also when processed food from big corporations didn't exist.

However, times have changed. Physical labour is decreasing and we don't burn off calories as easily. Hence, we need to monitor our food intake carefully. If a big part of our diet has to come from packaged food, we need to understand and label it accordingly.

Of course, nutritional information is provided on most packaged food products today. However, to the average person it is a jumble of tiny font text and numbers. Even if you were to read the data, what would you make of it? Is it healthy food or junk food? Or is it healthy but only in moderation?

Hence, we need a simple label for our food, comprehensible at a quick glance. This should be akin to the green and red dot for vegetarian and non-vegetarian food, which has worked well.

We need a new junk–healthy scale classification for all foods. One example, purely for illustration, is to use four tiny dots, in red or green, based on the junk–healthy scale. A red colour for all four dots would mean it is completely junk food. Chips, aerated drinks and fried snacks would belong here. Three red dots and one green would mean it is mostly junk, but perhaps not as high in fat, such as instant noodles or juices made from concentrate with added sugar. Foods that are healthy in small amounts, such as high-calorie nuts, would have two red and two green dots each. Mostly healthy but still processed foods, such as skim-milk packs and low-sugar juices would earn one red and three green dots. Four green dots would be reserved only for fresh, healthy and unprocessed foods such as fresh vegetables, low-calorie fruits and low-fat meats.

Only foods with three green dots or more would be allowed to advertise themselves as healthy. While this labelling will obviously not answer every nutritional question, it will at least tell consumers what kind of food they are eating.

The above four-dot template is just an example. However, junk versus healthy labelling is essential and implementable. This will increase awareness about what we are eating, and over time incentivize us as well as manufacturers to move towards healthier foods.

A healthy society leads to lower healthcare costs, improved productivity at work and a better quality of life for citizens. Food is a big part of public health. About time we knew what we are putting in our mouths.

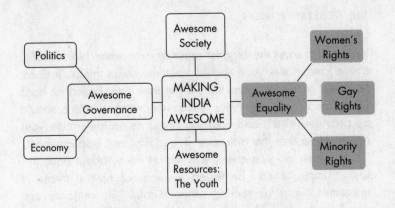

Politics

Awesome
Governance

Economy

Awesome
Society

MAKING
INDIA
AWESOME

Awesome
Resources:
The Youth

Awesome
Equality

Women's
Rights

Gay
Rights

Minority
Rights

AWESOME EQUALITY: WOMEN'S RIGHTS, GAY RIGHTS AND MINORITY RIGHTS

My dream, and the goal of this book, is not just Making India Rich. It is Making India Awesome. Being a developed nation, and therefore being a rich country, is part of being awesome. However, it isn't enough. To be awesome, one has to earn respect and coolness, something that doesn't come from money alone. Neither does it come from just military might, or any other kind of power. True coolness and respect comes from another aspect of a country—and that is providing fair treatment and equality. A society can be called equal when it doesn't matter who you are and where you come from. For no matter what, the land will treat you the same in terms of opportunity and justice.

No country is perfect in terms of equality. In human society, full equality is almost impossible. Communist-style experiments have failed, mainly because any communist regime often leads to an autocratic leadership, which controls everyone and ironically creates the biggest sense of inequality. No, equality doesn't mean everyone should have the same things. It does, however, mean everyone should get their due, based on hard work, merit and creativity. It also means that justice should be provided to all, and your identity does not determine your rights. Note that the aim here is equality, not appeasement.

So, how do you check if a nation cares about equality? Quite simply, it can be tested in terms of how it treats its minorities. In a democracy, theoretically, the majority can decide everything. It can even make minorities suffer, using a so-called completely democratic process. However, this is where the checks and balances of equality come in.

India has three main kinds of minorities—religious (non-Hindus), sexual (gays and lesbians) and gender (women). While non-Hindus and homosexuals are in a minority due to sheer numbers, women are considered a minority, given our historically male-dominated society.

How we treat these three minorities in the future will determine how awesome our nation becomes. Quite frankly, we have some way to go in achieving awesome levels. We still have Section 377, a legacy of the Victorian age, which criminalizes gay sex, a law so regressive, only a few orthodox religious states around the world have it today. We still don't treat our women right, and often deny them rights without even realizing it. And every now and then, the fear of communalism and actual violence against religious minorities makes them feel unsafe.

The sub-section on women's rights contains seven pieces which talk about how Indian women can actually empower themselves, and what we men need to do to support them. Many of the writings in this section had gone viral when they were previously published, often forwarded by women to each other as motivators. Thank you, ladies, for the same!

The sub-section on minority rights mainly talks about

Muslims, because they comprise the biggest religious minority in India. Again, the emphasis is on self-empowerment within the community and a desire to show the majority their point of view.

The essay on Section 377 was written to lend support to the gay rights groups. It talks about how these rights are important to all Indians, even if they are not gay.

They say that the test of a person's character is how he or she treats those less powerful than him or her. The test of a nation's character is how its majority citizens treat minorities. Equality is awesome. Let's keep working towards it.

WOMEN'S RIGHTS

Ladies, Stop Being so Hard on Yourself

> When you have reasonable expectations from yourself, you can be happy. And being happy is, above all else, having it all.

In this essay, I seek to address one women's issue—the belief that women can't really have it all.

This is an endless debate, which was fuelled into a storm in 2014 by Indra Nooyi, the chief executive officer (CEO) of Pepsi. It revolves around the issue of work-life balance, and the assertion that no woman can have a successful career and also manage family responsibilities well. Thus, for all the talk of women's empowerment, we as a society have not evolved to a point where women can have it all.

Do note that this issue, and therefore this piece, applies to a relatively small section of Indian women—those who actually have choices in terms of career options, or whether to work or not. Most women do not even have a choice of having it all. For them, it is more about keeping and preserving whatever they have.

Anyway, here is my take.

The phrase 'can't have it all' is a derivative of 'I am going to fail somewhere' or even 'something will prevent me from being fully happy'. The first phrase is right. The second is incorrect. Yes, you will fail at something. No, failing at something doesn't mean you can't be happy. The fear of failing is endemic in humans. In women, from what I have seen, the feeling is compounded multiple times with the constant belief that 'I am just not good enough'. Open any women's magazine—every page of every issue has tips on how to look, cook and make love better. I don't know if it is cultural, or if women come biologically wired like this, but they feel inadequate. It doesn't take much to reinforce that belief. A thinner neighbour, a schoolkid who gets a better tiffin box than your kids, a boss who praises a colleague instead of you—all set off loud inner alarms in women that scream, 'Look, you suck. Hence proved.' This feeling, in turn, leads women to have what I term the 'A+ complex'. This means in order to prove to themselves that they are not terrible, they must get an A+ in every department of life. As a mother, employee, boss, wife and dinner host, or even in terms of having a good figure, there is only one way to escape that feeling of being inadequate—get an A+.

How do you do that? Well, kill yourself, almost. Don't sleep, don't have time for yourself, let every jibe from any random person in the world affect you, don't think, react to the world that always seems to be demanding things from you, collect nuggets of praise along the way to keep fighting to avoid that feeling of inadequacy or dropping the ball. Cry alone at night, but don't ever let the world down. Keep repeating, 'Must go for A+ everyday, in everything, and all the time.'

Now tell me, can any person who thinks like that ever have it all?

No. They can't. Which is why women cannot have it all. The only thing they have lots of, as a result of this, is guilt. Women are guilty of not being a hundred per cent at office, not being there when their kids need homework help, not attending the mother-in-law's puja because there's a work trip, not going to the gym because they only get four hours of sleep every day.

Women, especially working women, feel so guilty that if, for some reason, they don't feel guilty for a day, they feel guilty about not feeling guilty. Get it? No? Neither do they.

So ladies, change just this one thing about you. Don't be so hard on yourself. Don't have the A+ complex. Overall, aim for a B+, or if you are a superwoman, an A- at best. Some days you will be an amazing A+ mom, but a B employee as you left work early. Other days you will be late from work and score an A+ there and the kids will have less of you, making you a B mom. But overall, if you score a B+, it is pretty good. That's better than many others and most of all, that is normal. Men do the same, and they don't go to bed thinking, 'Oh, I was an awful father today' or 'I didn't pay my dues to my employer'. They go to bed thinking, 'Well, let's not go there.'

So please don't kill yourself in trying to have it all. Just be normal, admit you won't be excellent at everything every day and smile through life.

When you have reasonable expectations from yourself, you can be happy. And being happy is, above all else, having it all.

I hope you like this essay. I am sure I could have written it better. But then again, I'm not aiming for an A+ anyway.

Five Things Women Need to Change about Themselves

> For all the talk of women being denied their proper place in society, ladies need to do some self-reflection too.

Dear Ladies,

A lot is said on how men should change, for us to respect our women better. Here are some suggestions: men need to see women as people, not objects. Men should realize and truly believe that women are as talented and capable as men and sometimes even more so. Men should not discriminate against women in the workplace or at home. Men have to respect boundaries and make sure their words do not make women feel uncomfortable. Men have to respect women's choices—in what they wear, where they want to go and at what time. Men should never use force or intimidation towards women.

Yes, we men have to learn. However, the stubborn, fragile and pampered Indian male ego is a tough nut to crack. Collectively we, as Indian men, have a long way to go before our women can be proud of us. We will. At least the process has started.

But in all this well-deserved male bashing, I hope the ladies do not miss out on another set of changes required, in themselves. Yes, for all the talk of women being denied their proper place in society, ladies need to do some self-reflection too.

Hence, I shall attempt the unthinkable. As a man, I will venture to give women advice. That alone is reason enough for me to be bashed to bits. However, every now and then, we men are prone to risk-taking behaviour. So forgive me, for I have dared.

Anyway, here goes. Five things I feel women need to change about themselves, to make things better for their own kind:

The first behaviour that needs to end is the constant desire to judge other women. Women are hard on themselves. They are harder on each other. An overweight woman enters the room. Most other women are thinking, 'How fat is she?' A working mother misses a parent-teacher (PTA) meeting due to an office deadline, others think what a terrible mother she is. A girl in a short skirt makes other women go 'Slut!' in their heads. A pretty woman's promotion makes other women wonder what she had been up to, to get the job. From an ill-fitting dress to a badly cooked dish, you are ready to judge others. This despite knowing you yourselves are not perfect. As a woman, it is tough enough to survive in a male-dominated world. Why be so hard on each other? Can you let each other breathe?

Second, the faking needs to end. A common female trait is the relatively quick adaptation to feed male egos. Laughing at men's jokes when they aren't funny, accepting a raw deal in an office assignment or playing dumb to allow a man to feel superior are just a few occasions when you do your own kind no favour. Who are you? And why can't you be that person? Why are you faking it so much? If something bothers you, say it. What's the point of collectively harping on equality when as individuals, you are happy to lapse into being clueless eye flutterers, just to keep men happy?

Three—and this is serious—standing up for your property rights. Plenty of Indian women give up their lawful property rights for their brothers, sons or husbands. Sorry if it sounds harsh, but too many Indian women are emotional fools and need to be told so. You are not demonstrating your eternal selflessness when you give away your property. You are hurting your own kind.

Four, women need to become more ambitious and dream bigger. All young Indians, men and women, should have fire in their bellies. Perhaps because of the way Indian society is structured, our women are not encouraged to be as ambitious as men. However, for their own sake and the nation's sake, all Indian youth must have ambitions and aspirations to do well and reach their maximum potential in life. Many Indian women have done much better than men. Use them as inspiration and work towards your dreams. Your success is what will finally make Indian men respect women. Play your part.

Five, don't get too trapped in the drama of relationships. Relationships are vital. Being a good mother, wife, sister, daughter, friend and lover are extremely important. However, don't get too tangled. You have another relationship, with yourself. Don't sacrifice so much that you lose yourself. Not regularly, but just every now and then, be a little selfish. It is when a woman will assert herself that she will be taken seriously. You are not here only to assist others in living their lives. You have your own life too.

I will end here. Hope you will see the point and intention behind what I am talking about. If not, then I am in big trouble!

Chetan Bhagat

Home Truths on Career Wives

> Choosing a capable, independent and career-oriented woman can also bring enormous benefits.

I remember watching the movie *Cocktail* in 2012, not so long ago. The plot revolves around a philanderer hero who has to make the tough choice between two hot women. The uber-modern movie was set in London. Two of the characters, the hero and one of the heroines, drink, dance in nightclubs and have one-night stands with aplomb. They work in new-age aspirational jobs like glamour photography, graphic art and software design. And yet, the guy eventually chooses the girl who cooks home food, dresses conservatively, wins his mother's approval and is happy to be the ideal Indian wife. In fact, even the rejected girl, a free-spirited, independent woman, agrees to change herself. To get the guy, she is happy to cook and change her lifestyle to match that of the ideal Indian wife.

While the movie was fun, such depictions disturb me a little. When successful, strong women are portrayed as finding salvation in making dal and roti for their husbands, one wonders what kind of India we are presenting to our little girls.

Really, is that what a woman's life is all about—to make hot phulkas? Of course, I shouldn't be so bothered, many would say. It is a Bollywood movie. The commercial pressure to present a palatable story is real. Above all, the makers have a right to tell the narrative they want.

Yet, when our most modern and forward cinema sinks into

regressive territory, it is unfair to our women. It is also depressing because deep down, we know such attitudes exist. Many Indian men, even the educated ones, have two distinct profiles of women—the girlfriend material and the wife material. One you party with, the other you take home. The prejudice against non-traditional women who assert themselves is strong.

Let us look at another part of the world. Yahoo, a leading tech firm and a Fortune 500 company, hired a female CEO in 2012, Marissa Mayer. What's more, she was six months pregnant when she was hired, a fact she did not hide in her interviews. Marissa took some time off after childbirth and got back to work later. She manages both her child and work, and was the highest paid female CEO in 2014, according to a *New York Times* list.* There is something to celebrate about that. Marissa is a role model for women and even men.

I'd like Indian men to have an open mind about choosing their life partners and revise their 'ideal woman' criteria. Having a traditional wife who cooks, cleans and is submissive might be nice. However, choosing a capable, independent and career-oriented woman can also bring enormous benefits. For instance, a man who marries a career woman gets a partner to discuss his own career with. A working woman may be able to relate better to organizational issues than a housewife. A spouse who understands office politics and can give you good advice can be an asset.

Two, a working woman diversifies the family income streams. In the era of expensive apartments and frequent lay-offs, a working spouse can help you afford a decent house and feel more secure about finances.

Three, a working woman is better exposed to the world.

---

*http://www.nytimes.com/interactive/2015/05/15/business/highest-paid-women-ceo.html?_r=0

She brings back knowledge and information that can be useful to the family. Whether it's the latest deals or the best mutual fund to invest in, or even new holiday destinations, a working woman can add to the quality of life.

Four, the children of a working woman learn to be more independent and will do better than mollycoddled children.

Five, working women often find some fulfilment in their jobs, apart from home. Hence, they may have better life satisfaction, and feel less dependent on the man. This in turn can lead to more harmony. Of course, all these benefits accrue if men are able to keep their massive, fragile egos aside and see women as equals.

Sure, there are drawbacks also in being with working women. But in the modern age that we live in, the phulka-making bride may come at the cost of missing out on other qualities. Please bear that in mind before you judge women based on their clothes, interest in the kitchen or the confidence in their voice.

My mother worked for forty years. My wife is the chief operating officer (COO) at an international bank. It makes me proud. She doesn't make phulkas for me. We outsource that work to our help, and it doesn't really bother me. If my wife had spent her life in the kitchen, it would have bothered me more.

Please choose your partner carefully. Don't just tolerate, but accept and even celebrate our successful women. They take our homes ahead and our country forward. We may not have hot phulkas, but we will have a better nation.

Wake up and Respect
Your Inner Queen

Every girl in India deserves a journey of
self-discovery like Rani.

Earlier, I had written about the movie *Cocktail* (2012). In that film—a modern, London-based love triangle—the free-spirited hero finally chooses a girl because she is more traditional. Of course, filmmakers have a right to make what they want. But the fact that our films needed to pander to such conclusions saddened me. It made me write about Indian men's inexplicable love for phulka-makers. I appealed to them to forsake hot phulkas and celebrate our working women, in the interest of the nation.

That aside, I had become resigned to the idea that Bollywood would never take a bold, liberal stance when it came to women. Even if a film dared to, the box office, comprising a conservative Indian audience, would punish it severely. I was happy—in fact, delighted—to be proved wrong. Last year, a fine film called *Queen* not only said what needed to be said, it also demolished old box-office expectations. It won the National Award for Best Hindi Film and the Best Actress award for Kangana Ranaut, both well deserved, as well.

The film, marketed as a fun entertainer, has done more for the feminist movement and women's empowerment than people will give it credit for. *Queen* is the story of Rani, a Punjabi girl from a conservative family living in West Delhi. Amazingly, like most Indian girls, she isn't even aware of the cloistered and confined life she is living. Her world view is limited to getting married, wanting the ceremonies to go well and ensuring that people dance enough. She seeks her husband's or parents' approval for most of life's decisions—from taking up a job to joining a college.

Dumped at the altar, Rani goes on a solo honeymoon to Paris and Amsterdam to get over her pain. On her first trip abroad, she befriends a free-spirited girl and shares a room with three male backpackers, all of different nationalities.

Her first exposure to the free world—a society where nobody questions you about your sexual, parenting and career choices—baffles her, but also becomes a coming-of-age lesson like none other. All her friends are somewhat dysfunctional, not-so-well-off and unsettled. They are everything Indian parents do not want their children to be. Yet, they seem happier with their lot than the well-settled life so many middle-class Indians aspire for. Suffice to say, Rani learns to stand up for herself and becomes a queen. She rejects the man who dumped her but is now stricken with remorse, even going so far as to thank him.

By Bollywood standards, the film has a highly unconventional ending. Yet, it worked with the audience. That alone is cause for celebration.

There are hidden messages in the movie, perhaps more than the makers even intended. One, we have trapped our women. We think we care for them, but we suffocate them in the name of security, safety, morality, tradition or culture. We are not comfortable with an Indian woman expressing herself. A woman has to be a good daughter, sister or wife. It isn't enough for her to be just, well, herself. In some ways, women endure disguised slavery. In the civilized, developed world, where women have choices, they do not choose to live like this. Every girl in India deserves a journey of self-discovery like Rani.

The film also shows us the need for India to integrate with the Western world. When are we going to do that? We are so lost in our caste and religion politics, so close-minded about anything foreign, so caught up in the duties society imposes on us, so pressurized to get marks and land a job, that we don't live as free and full a life as humans can. When did you hear of Indian students taking gap years after college to explore the world? How would we react if a girl says she wants to try out a few relationships before she settles down? In the name of preserving morals, we want to tie our women up. What has that led to? Where are there more rapes? Here in don't-date, don't-drink, don't-wear-modern-clothes India; not in Europe, where dating is a personal choice, alcohol is available at every corner store and people are free to wear swimsuits on beaches.

We need to ask some questions. Where have we gone wrong in our traditions and what do we need to change? We need to unshackle our women. We need to learn, connect and behave in tune with the free world. Not just Rani, not just women; but also all of us need to awaken and respect our inner Queen.

Indian Men Should Channelize Their Inner Mr Mary Kom

> Why is it that a husband who helps out in the kitchen and takes care of the kids is termed 'amazing', while when a woman does it, she is merely 'doing her job'?

While on the subject of movies, another wonderful film I saw was *Mary Kom*, a biopic based on our real-life champion boxer Ms M.C. Mary Kom. The film, helmed by Priyanka Chopra, had many things going right for it, and not just in the technical aspects, where everyone has done a fabulous job. Ms Kom's journey is fantastic material to begin with, and the film team did a great job in bringing the inspiring story to life.

Interestingly, the biggest challenges for the protagonist are outside the boxing ring. The hard parts aren't the punches in the face, but things like having your parents agree to your career choice; marriage; pregnancy and motherhood. The challenges of normal life that make it hard to chase a dream. The fact that Ms Kom trumped all this and won is what makes her an icon.

However, there is another star in the story. It is Mary Kom's husband, Onler Kom (played impeccably by Darshan Kumaar in the film), who becomes her rock-solid support at all times. From cheering her on in the boxing ring to changing diapers at home, Onler doesn't let Mary's dream die. He puts his career on the backburner, sends his wife to practise and rocks their twin infants to sleep. Not surprisingly, the endearing Mr Mary Kom won as many hearts in the audience as his spouse. Several girls in the audience swooned, 'What an amazing husband!' Everyone falling in love with Onler had me thinking. Mr Mary Kom was great, but isn't that what millions of Indian women do for their husbands every day, anyway? Say the movie was about a male boxer, with a supportive wife who took care of the kids—would we ever gush over her? Don't we all know couples where the wives' careers have taken a backseat so their husbands can do well instead? Why is it that a husband who helps out in the kitchen and takes care of the kids is termed 'amazing', while when a woman does it, she is merely 'doing her job'?

There was a time when jobs involved high manual labour and perhaps men were more suited to the workplace. Today, it is a different world. How many male readers of this article do a job that a woman can't do instead? And yet, when a woman sacrifices her dreams and career for a man, it is expected of her. When a man does it, the reaction is somewhere between 'Has he gone crazy?' to 'He is awesome'.

It is time all this changes. If India has to move ahead, we have to optimize our resources, and women are half of our human resources. We have to help them reach their full potential too. And it is about time we men awaken a little bit of Mr Mary Kom within ourselves.

How can we do that? Well, here are three ways you can be Mr Mary Kom, or a supportive husband.

One, listen to and see your wife as a human being first, not as a woman, wife or your parents' daughter-in-law. Your wife is an individual. And individuals have individual dreams, opinions, motivations and points of view. You may or may not agree with all of them, but are you at least aware of them? Your wife may want to reach the heights in her career, or she may want to completely be there for the kids, or perhaps she wants a good mix. Do you know what she wants? And how are you helping her achieve that?

Two, be fair in parenting responsibilities. And no, 'kids are your responsibility while I make the money' is not fair. Kids have two parents. You are one of them. You have to do your bit.

Three, strive to make your partner the best person she can possibly be. This need not be just career related. Maybe your wife has fitness goals, or wants to learn something, or improve her social relationships. Are you helping her? Is there a role you play in her life for achieving her dreams, even if it is to patiently listen to her insecurities?

The above suggestions are by no means exhaustive. A lot of being supportive is intuitive. However, it does take courage for an Indian man to truly be there for his wife. This is because our sexist society mocks men who back their wives, almost implying a sense of weakness in them. However, I hope the new Indian husband will not be so insecure. Being a supportive husband doesn't make you less of a man, or henpecked, or weak. It just makes you a better, cooler human being. And don't forget, any Mr Mary Kom is just as much of a champion as Ms Mary Kom.

Fifty Shades of Fair: Why Colour Gets under Our Skin

> We are not a fair-skinned race, and that is okay.

One thing that baffles me about India is our love for fair skin. Not unlike many African and Asian countries, Indians too obsess about having a lighter skin colour, consider people with lighter skin more beautiful and, in the worst case, even ascribe a higher status to them. From the multi-million-dollar fairness-products industry to the fact that all children in our baby-products ads are fair, one no longer needs to debate that Indians love lighter skin. We do, and that might have been just one of those many Indian quirks had it not had harmful societal impact. Indians are not fair-skinned on an average, and thus millions have a complex about their skin colour.

Women, in particular, bear the brunt of it. When growing up, I remember my darker-toned cousins being told to not drink tea (in the mistaken traditional belief that tea makes one dark, never mind the English never turned dark despite fighting wars for tea), or to study harder because they were dark and hence it would not be easy to marry them off. Apart from judgements about looks, there is something more onerous when it comes to skin colour and Indians. Dark-skinned people get fewer opportunities in India. This is not racism, but is sometimes referred to as colourism or pigmentocracy. Fair-skinned people are more likely to be hired in certain jobs (when was the last time you saw a dark-skinned flight attendant on an Indian airline?).

We must address this—but not by routine lip service or catchy slogans on Facebook. To address the issue, we need to understand the root cause driving this bias towards fair skin. The key reason is the associations related to colours, and also to people of a particular colour.

First, is it just the intrinsic colours? White. Black. What do these colours signify to you? White is often used in the context of clarity, purity and cleanliness. Black is used to describe the opposite. White is clean, black is dirty. Is some of this carried through when we refer to the same colours in the context of our skin?

Of course, not everything black is seen as unaesthetic. Thick and shiny black hair is associated with youth, health and beauty. Images of dark brown chocolate, associated with deliciousness, can make one's mouth water. The little black dress, which can accentuate one's figure, is considered beautiful. Hence, it isn't just the fundamental black and white colours that make us find one pretty and the other not so. It is what those colours are associated with. And here is the real reason why our minds are almost conditioned to prefer white skin.

A lighter skin is associated with European or Caucasian ethnicity. People from these countries are much richer and considered more successful on an average. They are also seen as happier. Their media and celebrities have a global impact and are considered aspirational. Darker-skinned people are associated with those who are poorer, work in the sun and are hence a couple of shades darker, perhaps even less educated and less aspirational. Hence, the skin colour of the aspirational becomes aspirational itself.

How to fix this? Well, awareness campaigns help, but only so much. What we need to change is to separate our aspirations from skin colour, as the latter has nothing to do with them. We also need to broaden our understanding of what is attractive in a person—is it just skin colour, or is it also things such as physical fitness, a charming personality and overall grooming? Stars like Rihanna or Will Smith are considered extremely attractive physically, even in the West. We need to fight our inherent low self-esteem, this sense of being ashamed of all things Indian, whether it is the vernacular language or the native skin colour. We are not a fair-skinned race, and that is okay. What matters is that we are capable, hard-working, progressive and compassionate. We also need to grow our economy and make our country rich so that this sense of shame goes away soon.

Be proud of who you are, country and colour included.

In reality, our skin is just our soft outer covering, no more than a couple of millimetres thick. Its main purpose is to protect our internal organs and aid sensation. In all this, the skin's colour has little relevance. What makes a person beautiful is much more than the outer wrapping we come in. Open your mind and discover it for yourself.

GAY RIGHTS

Section 377 Is Our Collective Sin

> This immoral law must go and we must drop our hypocrisy on homosexuality.

One thing we Indians are extremely good at is detaching ourselves from misery, injustice and conflict. We go about our lives as if India's big problems don't exist. I am not judging us. It is the only way to cope in a country with so much misery and inequality.

Another thing we are good at, as I discussed in my piece 'Let's Talk about Sex', is not discussing any problems that have a sexual angle. This is the reason why we still don't have reasoned, nuanced and rational debates on crimes against women and why many of us think sex education is a terrible thing.

In all this denial and hypocrisy we have buried and accepted a gross injustice that affects millions of Indians and clubs our nation with some of the most backward, regressive regimes in the world. It is the issue of gay rights, or the infamous Section 377, that still exists in our law books and criminalizes homosexuality. This, despite oodles of scientific evidence in the past decade about the existence of homosexuality as natural and almost all medical and scientific experts believing that there is nothing 'abnormal' or 'incorrect' about being gay.

How many people does it affect? Well, homosexual populations are around 20 per cent across the world* (another

---

*http://www.nber.org/papers/w19508

data point to show that this is indeed a natural, consistent occurrence, not caused by cultural or societal factors). We label around 100 million Indians as criminals and go about our daily lives as if their concerns are irrelevant to us. To me, this is nothing short of a collective sin.

Why is this happening? What can be done about it? And why should we, the selfish, acche-din and GDP-growth-seeking Indians care?

Homosexuality is a complex issue, with science unfortunately not being the only basis on which people have an opinion on it. There are religious, moral, political and legal standpoints involved. However, one thing is screamingly clear—there is enough reason to not criminalize homosexuality from any of these standpoints.

Scientific evidence shows that homosexuality exists in nature. From a religious point of view, the orthodox stance is anti-homosexuality, but many denominations of several religions accept or are neutral towards it. In Hindu religion, the stance ranges from positive to neutral to antagonistic. The Rig Veda says 'Vikruti Evam Prakriti' (perversity/diversity is what nature is all about, or what seems unnatural is also natural).

Morally, while you may argue that men and women are supposed to be attracted to each other and everything else is immoral, isn't it also immoral to take away someone's free will? Isn't it immoral to call their preference a perversion without listening to the gay point of view? Isn't it immoral to force a gay person to marry someone of the opposite sex and make him or her live a fake life? Isn't it immoral to crush the gay movement simply because gays are a minority?

Accepting gay rights is only being sensitive to the genuine needs of a discriminated community. On that note, I would have one suggestion for the gay community. We live in a conservative country that needs to change, but change happens slowly. Any breakthrough in gay rights should not spill out on the streets, in the form of Western-inspired gay parades or anything that presents being gay as being somewhat fashionable or cool. While you have the right to do so, please note that we have to nudge a conservative, almost hostile society towards change. If we freak them out, they will only withdraw further.

Politically, there are a lot of conservative voters who vote for the BJP. While many BJP seniors are pro-decriminalization, they cannot go public about it, lest opponents take political advantage of it. However, conservative BJP voters are also the most loyal BJP voters. While a section of them may be upset with the move, they really have no choice to vote for anyone else at the moment.

Which brings us to the last standpoint of legality. Section 377 is not an Indian law but an inheritance of British law. The same law, with the same section number, existed in over forty colonies of the British empire. Most of them have junked it or modified it to decriminalize homosexuality. We have held on to it as if it is part of India's cultural heritage, whereas it is nothing but a relic of an unscientific Victorian past.

Of course, the final question is this: why should the selfish, non-homosexual, growth-seeking Indian care? Well, we should. Countries where minority rights are protected, moral viewpoints are more modern and liberal and laws change with the times to reflect global best practices and scientific discoveries, tend to do better in terms of income growth. Most developed and free nations of the world accept homosexuality, as they should.

If we want to be one of them one day, it is time to start behaving like we belong in the modern world. Strong minority rights are evidence of justice in society. They show even the powerless are heard and protected. With justice comes a higher sense of investor confidence, which in turn leads to higher economic growth. So, gay or not, we need to do this. We need to remove Section 377. We need to move ahead in the world.

MINORITY RIGHTS

Letter from an Indian Muslim Youth

> The Indian Muslim has evolved.
> It is time you do too.

Dear Caretakers of Indian Muslims (this includes secular parties, once-communal parties, confused allies, maulvis, Muslim welfare organizations and generally anybody these days),

You are probably wondering who I am. After all, I don't have a name like Ahmed or Saeed or Mirza, anything that will clearly establish me as a Muslim. You forget, this writer also writes fiction. So perhaps I, and what I say here, is nothing but a fabrication. However, maybe there's something useful in there for all you well-wishers.

Everyone seems to care for Muslims, but no one actually wants to listen to us, particularly the youth. I keep hearing political leaders promising to uplift us. I don't know how they plan to uplift us and only us without uplifting the nation. But then I am a nobody; what do I know?

I see them wear Muslim caps, perhaps to show us that they really do mean to improve our lives. However, a cap on your head doesn't change anybody's life. Using what's inside your head might. You haven't. For why else do we continue to be one of the most backward communities in India?

It is not like India has a shortage of Muslim achievers. There are Muslim stars in almost every field. These people achieved what they did without any cap-wearing politician helping them. They had a modern outlook and a desire to come up in life. We need a leader who understands this, and inspires us to do better. We need jobs. We need good schools and colleges. We need good, clean homes with power and water. We need a decent standard of living. We don't need it as a handout. We are willing to work hard for it. Just, if you can, create the opportunities for us to do so.

What makes you think that all a leader has to do is wear a cap, dole out some freebies, speak empty words and expect us all to vote in a pack? What are we, a herd of sheep? Does the God we pray to make us all part of one flock when it comes to politics? Is that India? Last I heard, we were not a religious republic. We are a democratic republic. So treat us like democratic citizens.

You know what hurts? We do not have a strong modern Indian Muslim voice. If I am an Indian Muslim, who believes in ambition, a scientific way of thinking, entrepreneurship, empowerment, progress and personal freedom, where do I go? Which party is backing that? Can someone give me a leader who represents my aspirations?

I cannot tell you the frustration we feel. It is bad enough that we find it difficult to rent an apartment, the police frisks us with greater attentiveness and we have to bear the occasional jibes. But what is truly sick is this: you guys claim to care for us but are only reinforcing that we are backward and doomed to remain so. Because of you, people feel that we vote in a herd and are keeping India backward. You, our caretakers, have led people to think we care only about religion and not about corruption and development. It isn't true. Corruption is stealing, and stealing is a sin. No true Muslim or progressive Indian can support it. Don't hide your sins behind your fake caring for us.

We know you neither care for India, nor for Islam.

Maybe I am being too harsh, and some of you are indeed well intentioned. But realize the consequences every time you slot us according to our religion. There is more to us than that.

If you truly want to help, there is one area where you could. We have a wonderful religion. However, like any religion, the interpretation of it can be orthodox or liberal. In many parts of the world, there's an extremely strict interpretation of Islam in daily life. India is more liberal, and many Muslims would prefer to keep it this way. Can you support us in that? Don't let our religious heads, extreme voices and fundamentalists control our lives, for that isn't the essence of India. If you can do that, we will back you. You will truly be our representatives if you promote real progress—through empowerment and modernization of our community. The Indian Muslim has evolved. It is time you do too.

Being Hindu Indian or
Muslim Indian

> India's influencers, intelligentsia and those who care for society across religions need to talk and work [religious] issues out.

One is always apprehensive about writing on religion. Most Indians don't discuss it in public, fearing misinterpretation. The only people who talk about religion are passionate extremists. Consequently, in our society, extremists control our religion and politics panders to this.

Important religious issues are ignored in the process. One such issue is the confusion that exists in the minds of youth about interpreting their own religion and its place in modern society.

Let us begin with Hinduism. There is a section of Hindus who believe in mutilating themselves to please the gods. They poke their cheeks with javelins. They pull chariots with metal hooks dug into their backs. Hindu sadhus live the lives of ascetics. Meanwhile, millions of Hindus go to the temple only occasionally. They believe in God. However, they neither follow nor are aware of every guideline given in the Hindu scriptures. Many Hindus eat meat and consume alcohol, but also pray to God and celebrate the major festivals.

So let's pose a question—what is a Hindu supposed to be? Is the cheek-poking devotee a benchmark? Is a sadhu the ideal

Hindu? Or is a regular middle-class person, working in a bank, eating chicken, drinking beer and occasionally visiting a temple, also a good Hindu?

Obviously, there is no clear answer. Everyone in the examples above is a Hindu. So what does it mean to be a Hindu in India? We can only guess, but here's an attempt at a list of modern Indian Hindu values.

The modern Hindu prays to Hindu gods and celebrates a few Hindu festivals. He follows at least a few of the Hindu practices, which vary from person to person. He does not impose his beliefs, rituals and faith on anyone else and is tolerant of others' beliefs. He ignores regressive tenets in our holy texts suggestive of gender inequality, caste discrimination or violence.

This list is neither exhaustive nor accurate, for we have never intellectually discussed what it means to be a Hindu in twenty-first-century India. The final list can emerge only after intensive debate. However, such a list is needed, as it attempts to build a practical consensus on religion's place in our society.

We also need to ensure that this list not only follows what the religion prescribes, but is also aligned with the aspirations and progress of the country as a whole. If we went back to the strict orthodox Hinduism practised in the sixteenth century, for instance, it would hamper us from being part of today's globalized world.

Similar discussions and listing of values are needed for other religions, particularly the other main Indian religion—Islam. There are nearly fifty countries in the world where Muslims are in a majority. However, there is no one interpretation of Islam.

For instance, take Saudi Arabia, where Muslims comprise almost 100 per cent of the population. The Saudi legal system does not work on a separate Constitution, but involves a strict, conservative interpretation of Sharia law. Examples of Saudi laws include the need for women to cover up in public, a woman's testimony being invalid (or carrying much less weightage than that of a man) and punishments such as beheading, lashing and stoning for a variety of crimes.

The laws are imposed strictly. During a fire at a Saudi school, the firemen allegedly did not let girls leave the burning building because they were not adequately covered. The girls died. Many criticize the Saudi system, while others praise it for low crime rates.

Let us take one more example, of Turkey. Striving for European Union membership, Turkey grants significant personal freedom to its citizens. Religion and politics are separate. A secular Constitution governs the legal system. Astonishingly, despite an almost 99 per cent Muslim population, wearing the hijab is banned in universities and public or government buildings (although this has recently been relaxed) as some view it as a symbol of religion, which needs to be separated from state institutions.

Other Muslim-majority countries are somewhere in the middle. Malaysia is somewhat liberal, Iran isn't, Pakistan is in the middle, etc. Which brings us back to the same question— who is more or less Muslim in the above examples?

Obviously there is no one right answer. What we do know is that a Turkish Muslim is expected to behave differently from a Saudi Muslim. So let us ask this question. Which example should Indian Muslims follow? Should they be like Turkish Muslims, Saudi ones or somewhere in the middle?

I will not attempt an answer, as it is not my place to do so. The answer will come from the community itself, keeping in mind the following—where do we want Indian society to go? Do we want to progress and create a nation where our youth can meet their aspirations? Are we fine with regressive and violent interpretations of our religious texts? Or is it okay if we selectively choose what works best for our society?

Such debates are required, but are sadly missing, as they are discouraged by our divisive politicians. India's influencers, intelligentsia and those who care for society across religions need to talk and work these issues out. If we do not, extremists will continue to hijack our religious debates, and divisive politicians will keep exploiting the confusion, much to the peril of the nation.

It's Not Moderate Muslims' Fault

> It is simple to blame educated, modern Muslims, as if they could somehow end the mindlessness that is going on in the name of their religion.

Inhuman terror attacks from fundamentalist Islamic organizations over the years have sent tremors round the world. As a scared world dissects the causes and tries to find solutions, many stress the role of the 'moderate Muslim', or educated and modern Muslims, who have kept quiet or not spoken up enough in all this.

However, it isn't that simple. To find solutions, it is important not to assign blame to a whole group of people. The first step is to try and understand the moderate Muslim point of view.

Imagine this. You have grown up respecting a religion and its holy texts. Along with customs and rituals you have also affirmed a lot of positive values—compassion, honesty, humility, love, integrity, generosity. You are a rational, scientific human being but still give religion an important place in your life. After all, it teaches you humanity, makes you a better person and keeps you positive.

Now imagine a small section of people, who claim to share your religion, spreading hate and violence. They claim to be defending the same religion you love and respect, but their actions do not agree with your conscience at all. This fringe group is a paradox. It upholds something you love, but acts in a manner you despise.

The actions of these people involve killing innocents including kids, brutalizing women or bombing and gunning down people. Soon, this fringe group grabs headlines. Your religion gets associated with terror, hate, intolerance and violence. Even though people from other religions don't say it, you can feel their prejudice towards you. With every incident, your religion gets more tainted.

You try to avoid the mess, going about your normal life as a moderate. But soon, you are blamed too. You are blamed for keeping quiet. You are blamed for having a soft spot for terrorists. You are blamed for not screaming loud enough to shut the fringe down.

That, unfortunately, is the predicament of the vast majority of Muslims today. The 'moderate Muslim' or the 'peace-loving Muslim' watches haplessly as on the one hand fundamentalists on the fringe damage the religion's image, and on the other, non-Muslims accuse them of not doing enough.

What is a moderate Muslim to do?

The answer is not easy. It is simple to blame educated, modern Muslims, as if they could somehow end the mindlessness that is going on in the name of their religion. But if others were to put themselves in Muslim shoes, they would realize their choices are limited.

If, for instance—and God forbid—Hindu radical groups had millions of dollars in funding, there were a dozen-plus countries which were officially Hindu nations, the rulers of these nations backed the radicals somewhat and the radicals were not afraid to use extreme violence, what could a modern, liberal, educated or, in other words, 'moderate' Hindu do?

Well, chances are the moderate Hindu would stay away from all this, and go about his own life, trying to raise his or her family in peace. It doesn't mean that the moderate Hindu supports radical groups, is intrinsically backward or doesn't care. However, the natural human instinct for self-preservation kicks in and not reacting seems the only way out.

The same happens with millions of moderate Muslims, who get disturbed by acts of terror as much as others do. They love their religion and so they cocoon themselves from such heinous acts by forming their own relationship with God.

The bigger question is, what can be done? What do we do to end acts that can only be described as medieval and barbaric, except that they are happening in this day and age?

Well, first, we have to stop finding sections of people to dump blame on. It is not about a particular religion. It is also not about a particular religious text prescribing more violence, as some analysts have suggested. All religious texts can be selectively interpreted in different ways. The Bible teaches compassion, but also has a lot of violence. The Gita's famous saying 'a virtuous war must be fought' can be seen as justifying violence, as what a radical group finds 'virtuous' is slippery terrain. The reason why this interpretation isn't made more often is that Hindu radical groups don't have as much power as Muslim radical groups do around the world at present.

The issue is not a particular religion or a particular text; the issue is fringe radical groups of a particular religion amassing great financial, military, political and media power. This power needs to be curbed, in whatever way possible, with a different strategy for each kind of power.

For this, sane voices from all nations and all religions must come together. This is the kind of issue the United Nations (UN) and North Atlantic Treaty Organization (NATO) should deal with together. It requires an organization equivalent to the UN for all the world's religions, backed by world leaders. In fact, it is amazing that we have no high-profile body that unites religions worldwide and takes up common issues facing all faiths.

These are all big demands. However, it will take time to fix one of the biggest problems in the world: radical religious terror. We, as humans, have not done enough to unite the world's religions. It is time we did.

Mapping the Route to
Minority Success

> Our minorities are not minor; they are
> an important part of India. In their success
> lies India's success.

There are writings that get you into trouble, and this might just be one of them. However, some things must be said simply because too many hypocrites have run the minorities agenda for too long. The results are there for all to see.

While many individual success stories exist, Muslims, the largest minority in India, are still well below the national average in terms of income, education and levels of influence in society. It isn't easy for Muslims to live in a society that discriminates against them. However, even many so-called 'keepers' of Muslim causes (the same ones who will attack me on this piece) have done little for the community other than suggestions such as: 'Never vote for the BJP, always vote for Congress.'

Such oversimplification and politicization has done more harm than good. It pains me to see a talented community being represented by regressive, parochial and divisive leaders who, frankly, do not care about India or its youth, and therefore, don't care about the Muslim youth either. With the intent of getting through to some positive-thinking, open-minded people, I give some suggestions.

Take a leaf out of the book of other successful communities.

The Jews in America and the Parsis and Sikhs in India are examples of minorities that have done extremely well in their respective countries. Jews form less than 2 per cent of the American population, but dominate lists of Forbes billionaires, Nobel laureates, media moguls and Hollywood bigwigs. How did this happen? Several theories abound. However, some factors seem firmly in place.

- Learning pays: The greater the emphasis on education, the greater the likelihood that members of a community will be successful.
- Assimilating with the majority community: Assimilation does not mean abandoning one's culture, or bending to the majority. It simply means finding as much common ground as possible. It also means not heeding leaders who are encouraging people to vote along communal lines. Even if one ignores the rights and wrongs of communal voting, it is not a productive strategy. Instead, Muslims need to put forth a checklist—a set of conditions—on what it would take for them to trust the BJP again. They mustn't just oppose the BJP. They must also hold out the possibility of supporting it if their conditions are met. Keeping all political parties on their toes and lobbying for your own cause is perfectly acceptable and even necessary. However, taking permanent sides is not. Please note, this doesn't mean that Muslims should vote for the BJP. It just means they should try to engage with the party rather than shun it completely. There is another important point about assimilation. It can't happen without trust, and assuming the best of people. It is understandably difficult to trust when that trust has been broken in the past. However, successful minority communities have been able to do that and have allowed the wounds to heal. Politicians often scare minorities, making

them believe the worst of people. It isn't a great way to live. Hope for, and spread, as much goodness as possible in your lifetime.

- Accepting liberal values and personal liberties: Most minority communities that have done well have also represented the liberal cause. This helps increase influence in society for a simple reason: most intellectuals are liberal. The youth, too, are attracted to liberal values. If you have intellectuals and the youth on your side, you already have disproportionate influence as compared to your actual population. Thus, the ultraconservative and orthodox interpretation of religion will not find as much traction as a modern, open-minded approach. Indian Muslims are more liberal than Muslims in many Islamic countries. Such voices should be encouraged.

- Encouraging merit: As a shortcut to appease Muslims, too many politicians have been suggesting quotas and waivers for the community. What makes communities rise is their talent and merit, not handouts. Reservations on offer are minuscule. However, they tag the community as in need of grace marks and antagonize the majority. They aren't worth it. Rise with education, hard work, creativity and business acumen. There really is no other way.

Our minorities are not minor; they are an important part of India. In their success lies India's success. About time we focused on what would enable them to be successful.

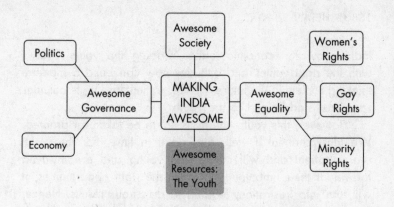

AWESOME RESOURCES: THE YOUTH

The main reason I became popular as an author was because the youth endorsed my work. They read my books, gave them word-of-mouth publicity and soon they even started listening to and reading my views outside of my stories. The youth, thus, have made me and it is for them that I write. In most cases, I represent their point of view in my writings, no matter what the topic. The title of this book also came from them. It is the youth that mostly use the term 'awesome'. Even though it is used as slang, I found it perfect to communicate the kind of India we need to aspire to.

The youth, however, are not just a demographic. They aren't just a target audience. They are a huge resource available to the nation. For almost every young citizen has dreams, energy and a willingness to put in the efforts to make it big in life. If we can channel this energy of over half a billion people towards making India shine, how awesome the results could be!

Tapping into the youth is a vital step towards making

India grow in economic terms. Shaping the youth's views with the right values and attitudes now can build a modern-thinking society in the future. Hence, sometimes I write columns specifically addressed to the youth.

However, this youth energy is not to be taken for granted. We must channel it well, and do it in time. For the youth are impatient and will not remain young and dreamy-eyed forever. If their ambition isn't given the right opportunities, it will turn into frustration, leading to disastrous results. Hence, our best resource is not only perishable, but if not utilized, could turn toxic.

Therefore, paying attention to this resource has to be any politician's top priority. We, as citizens, must judge politicians on the same. Education and jobs, important to the youth, have to be improved and created at a rapid pace.

'An Open Letter to Indian Change Seekers' talks about the need to be inclusive in order to really change society, something the youth must understand. In 'We, the Half-educated People', I have discussed the sad state of the quality of primary education. 'DU-ing It All Wrong, Getting It All Mixed Up' is about the problems in Delhi University's cut-off system. 'How the Youth Can Get Their Due' tells the youth to organize themselves into a vote bank. 'Scored Low in Exams? Some Life Lessons from a 76-Percenter' tries to advise students who have scored low marks in the boards on what to do next.

India is its youth. If the youth are awesome, nothing can stop the nation from being awesome.

An Open Letter to
Indian Change Seekers

If you want change, be inclusive.

Dear Change Seekers,

You have worked hard to make India a safer place. In 2012–13, the Delhi gang rape dominated headlines and received worldwide attention, mainly due to your efforts. However, be mindful of certain worrisome negative aspects of this outrage. You may create a lot of noise, but not the desired change. It is important to understand India first.

India, no matter what your civics teacher told you, is not an equal country. India is divided into four classes with different levels of power. For simplicity, let us call these classes the Ones, the Twos, the Threes and the Fours (deliberately avoiding upper–lower classification).

The Ones are our political masters. They control India, primarily through control over land, resources and the laws that govern us. They don't directly own assets, but control the asset owners, the Twos.

The Twos are our industrialists and capitalists. They help secure and increase the power of the Ones. Business magazines honour them with terms like 'the dynamic entrepreneurs of a new, liberalized India'. While some may deserve such accolades, most don't. The Ones allow the Twos to become rich through limited competition and tightly regulated approvals. Real estate, mining, infrastructure and most other sectors—no company in India can thrive without the support of the political class.

The next class, the Threes, is of people like you and me. We are people with a certain amount of affluence and education, comprising around 10 per cent of India's population. While life is a struggle for many Threes, they do have a basic standard of living. However, the Threes still do not get speedy justice, accountable leaders or a protective police force.

Notably, the Threes have recently acquired a new media power. They are affluent and buy things advertisers want to sell. Hence, the media caters to the Threes. The Threes dominate social media too. This power is real and substantial.

The Delhi bus gang rape victim was a Three, and the gruesome case made the rest of the Threes feel vulnerable like never before. They wanted the rape to be debated. Hence, for almost a month, little else could be discussed in a country of over 1.2 billion people. However, in the process, the Threes might have done some damage. For, despite the well-intentioned outcry, they inadvertently showed that they care about themselves much more than another huge class, the Fours.

The Fours make up 90 per cent of the country, people with limited education, abysmal standards of living and little hope for a better future. They are our farmers, slum dwellers, domestic helpers and the hundreds of millions of Indians without proper healthcare, education and infrastructure. They get no debates on TV. People won't protest for them at India Gate. The Threes either shun them, or impose their new-found modern values on them. For example, the Fours may see women–men relationships in a regressive way. The Threes, exposed to the latest Western beliefs, will mock them.

If you noticed the various debates and opinions on the gang rape case, the Threes only accepted ideas in line with their own liberal, modern value system. Nobody could dare say anything even slightly alternative or stress the Indian reality without being ridiculed.

The Threes found a new power, but used it like the Ones and Twos—for self-serving purposes.

For will we ever passionately discuss the issues and lend our media power to issues that affect the Fours? Will we go to India Gate to help slum dwellers get proper drinking water, for instance?

As we alienate the Fours, we leave them open to be exploited by the Ones. The Ones echo the sentiments of the Fours and throw some scraps at them. In return, the Fours ignore the Ones' misdeeds and bring them back to power. Meanwhile, we Threes keep screaming and watch our own self-created reality show.

This is no way to create a revolution, or even change. We have to take the Fours along. If we want people to change, we should not mock or deride. Instead, listen and understand first, and slowly nudge people towards change. Don't just laugh at anyone who says women should cover up and not venture out at night. Suggest that while this old belief may come from a place of practical reality, this cannot be the primary solution. I am not saying these people are not regressive. However, if you want change, be inclusive.

India's poor are not a separate species from us. If the politicians didn't protect the Twos so much, we could open the economy further, truly liberalize and create a lot of opportunity.

Chetan Bhagat

We, the Half-educated People

> Children are the future of the republic,
> but our schools are failing them.

I would like to draw your attention to something important that happened at the beginning of the year 2015. A significant survey was released in January with major implications for the future of our republic, even as it got lost amongst the politics served hot by TV channels.

Called the Annual Status of Education Report or ASER 2014, it is the tenth such survey. Facilitated by the NGO Pratham and conducted by local district-level organizations, ASER is the largest, most comprehensive annual household survey of children in rural India. ASER 2014 reached 16,497 villages and about 570,000 children were covered.

First, the good news. Enrolment levels in schools are 96 per cent. Most of our kids go to school now. The other good news includes a functioning midday meal programme (in over 85 per cent of schools) and improved infrastructure. Around 75 per cent of rural schools have drinking water while 65 per cent have toilets, significantly higher than five years ago.

However, the biggest concerns arise from what is actually happening inside the schools. Which is to say, how the schools do in terms of what they are meant to do—teach students.

Detailed results are available online, but here are three quick data points: half the kids in class five cannot read simple sentences that are taught in class two in urban schools. Half the kids in class five cannot do the basic two-digit subtraction, which is taught in class two. Half the kids in class eight cannot do the simple division that is taught in class four in private schools.

There you go. Half of our school students, after spending six years in school, cannot read basic sentences or perform simple arithmetic. The same could have been learnt within two to three years in a good urban private school.

So what are we doing in our rural schools, and what kind of talent are we creating? Are we simply going to celebrate enrolment and midday meal figures, and forget about a school's core job—to educate? What is literacy anyway? Is it just being able to write one's name, or is it, at a minimum, being able to read and solve basic arithmetic problems?

Why are basic reading and arithmetic vital? Because almost all education in subsequent years assumes these skills. Adding more years of education to such students will be a waste. Data shows that if basic skills are not learnt well early, they won't be learnt later, nor would anything advanced. These students will be the laggards, counted in our enrolment but eventually not getting educated.

If this were a small percentage of students, we could live with it. That it is more than half our students shows a major failure in our educational system. This can be changed. It is fixable, provided we first realize the gravity of the problem and then prioritize it in government.

Sadly, our so-called intellectual and political debates have been reduced to personality contests. With no known face attached to this problem we don't care much, hence the media ignores it as well.

However, these millions of kids and their families are being cheated and short-changed by us. We, the well-educated, frankly don't give a damn about rural kids, as they are too different from people like us. However, if we don't fix the problem, we will have hundreds and millions of hungry, job-seeking youth with little qualification and no educated world view in the next decade or two. If we don't want this time bomb of human mediocrity to explode on us, let us work on reforming rural education now.

Here are some workable ideas.

First, use technology. There is a shortage of good teachers, but if we bunch up a few schools in the same area and use a combination of virtual classes (conducted by more senior teachers) and physical classes (with less skilled teachers), we can have significant efficiency gains. A national classroom won't work, given that early education requires individual attention. But local clustering using technology will work well.

Second, have reporting systems. Opening a school and admitting students is not enough. Like any service provider, it needs to run well on a daily basis. Tracking actual changes in skill levels of kids, rather than counting heads in the building, will go a long way. For this, centralized technology can be used.

Third, change the class- and grade-based system. The class one to class twelve system may not work so well for the early years. Unless a student has basic skills, he or she should not be sent to higher classes. While nobody wants to stress little kids with exams and tests, we have to create hurdle markers based on actual learning in the early years.

Fourth, modify the course content. Our course materials are dated. The rote learning we subject our kids to not only prevents grasp of a concept, it allows students to keep moving up the system despite not gaining any real skills of comprehension or logic.

These are just a few suggestions. Many brilliant minds in the country can suggest more. Solutions will come, but what is needed is a desire among citizens to address what is important, rather than what is sensational. More than half our students are not even being half-educated. Now, does this deserve our full attention or not?

DU-ing It All Wrong, Getting It All Mixed Up

> When admission comes down to minor differences in marks, it becomes almost irrelevant.

Yet another college admission season in Delhi University (DU) has wound up. We saw the usual news stories about insanely high cut-offs. DU officials came on TV and talked about how there are still some seats available in random courses. Weekend supplements carried articles on how to reduce stress on the child and the family as a whole, and how failure doesn't really matter (even though newspapers celebrate success all year long). Soon, we saw the customary second, third and fourth lists, and the gates closed.

A tiny fraction of students who scored near-perfect marks in their board examinations made it inside the DU fortress. The rest twiddled their thumbs or settled for one of the many private colleges that spend more money on television ads than on real research and academics. As soon as the season ends, we will go back to our stories of scams and communal politics. Even though the cycle is sure to be repeated next year. For now, we have chosen our best students and future leaders.

Or have we? It doesn't take a PhD scholar to tell you a student who scores 96 per cent is unlikely to be much worse than a 98-percenter who gets the seat. In fact, the 96-percenter may well be better, as the scores are for one set of exams conducted for a limited range of topics. The more insane the cut-offs become, the less the difference between the students who are selected and those rejected. And yet we continue with this practice, ignoring a child's talent, personality, communication skills, his or her ability to work in teams, motivation, dreams, vision, imagination, creativity, values, convictions and opinions.

Anyone with substantial life experience would point out that board marks are hardly a major determinant of future success. When admission comes down to minor differences in marks, it becomes almost irrelevant.

Let us take two examples. Say, Student A is the head of a debating society, volunteers at an NGO several hours a week, can play a musical instrument and has fought a difficult family situation to educate herself. She scores 87 per cent. Student B has never done any extra-curriculars, finds it difficult to speak in groups and has spent most of his life poring over textbooks. Student B scores 94 per cent. Hence, Student B will get the seat in DU, but Student A won't.

Does this seem fair? Are we not being too reductionist in our approach to evaluating our best? Are we not incentivizing our students to shun developing a personality and other interests? Aren't we turning them into a mad, possessed herd focused only on scoring the maximum marks? Is it any surprise that most corporates complain that new recruits lack all-round personality and communication skills? Who will change this? Shouldn't DU take the lead?

The US, for instance, has an elaborate admission process for its top colleges. The selection is based on academics, essays, extra-curriculars, recommendations and achievements outside the classroom. It is no less draconian, mind you. And this write-up is not to make a case for lowering standards. It is merely to redefine what those standards are, especially at the top colleges. This impacts not only the students who finally get in, but also influences the rest who aspire to enter them. How our best colleges choose will influence how the next tier performs, and so on and so forth.

Until we go ahead with these reforms, all this talk of 'there is more to life than marks' will ring hollow. If there is indeed more to life, change the admission process. Make it more all-round, more subjective and choose people who deserve to be leaders in society.

A word of caution here, with respect to the word 'subjective'. The moment anything is made subjective in India, nepotism creeps in. The brutal cut-offs may have many flaws, but the 'highest marks gets in' criterion reduces the scope for manipulation. Given how our country works, it is quite likely that nephews, nieces and neighbours of admission committee officials will be seen as extraordinary all-round candidates. Any reform must ensure the new admission process is just as accountable, even though subjective. The army does it, the Union Public Service Commission (UPSC) does it and B-schools also have multiple criteria. There is no reason DU cannot do it, perhaps with the help of independent advisers.

An expansion of DU should also be on the cards. DU-II and DU-III campuses, in Gurgaon and Greater Noida, would be perfect. The number of students applying has multiplied, while reputed colleges have not. The Indian Institutes of Technology (IIT) have tripled their seats in the last decade, so why not DU?

A strong talent identification and promotion system is essential for a progressive society. We've not focused on it enough, leading to a warped education system. Let not another admission season go to waste.

How the Youth Can Get Their Due

> A rich, prosperous India should be every Indian's dream.

I went to a restaurant once where a waiter, a young boy of twenty-two, gave me the best service. It wasn't a particularly upscale establishment, but the waiter spoke perfect English. He kept up a smile through his gruelling job. People gave him customizations on every order, he listened with patience and kept track. He had a good IQ and had completed his graduation. This was the best job he could find.

His salary: ₹8,000 a month, in Mumbai. That is $120 a month, more than half of which would go in renting a shared room, an hour's commute away.

It broke my heart, and not for the first time. I have met, over the past few years, hundreds of talented, well-qualified youngsters across India, who do not have the kinds of jobs they deserve and are capable of. I could not enjoy my meal, wondering, what did this kid do wrong? Why was his monthly salary lower than one day's minimum wage in the US?

You see them everywhere. They help you try on T-shirts in a posh store. They man the cash counters in food courts of swish malls. They pick up the phone when you dial call centres. The typical profile is a youth from small-town India, whose parents spent their life savings educating him or her, and this is the best job the youth could find.

With the same qualifications and same amount of work, they could make much more abroad. Why is it that we can't give them the same opportunity?

These millions of youth across the nation drive my politics. Unfortunately, the kind of politics we have practised and the governments that have resulted have ensured that we suffocate the talents of an entire generation.

We have spent our time arguing who is secular and who is not, who cares for Dalits better, who is the beacon of goodness and who is absolute evil. Of course, much of this is nonsense. No one community in India can uplift itself much until the country as a whole rises. Teaching each other a lesson for historical wrongs is not going to help the youth get their due.

Also, there is no party that is completely clean and pure, as it is impossible to run politics like that. Even if not monetarily corrupt, all parties make fake promises to poor people that they know they cannot fulfil.

Still, we waste so much time discussing what is inconclusive and irrelevant. Switch on political news on television and you will see nothing but attacks, counter-attacks and charges. In all this, how do the youth get their due?

Well, they can, if they realize their power and begin to vote on the right issues. The number one issue right now is the economy. If we don't grow at 10 per cent per year, we will not be able to provide enough jobs for the youth.

Without sufficient growth, we will also not have enough tax revenues to pay for all the infrastructure projects, healthcare and education the country needs to spend on. Money, even though considered morally inferior on the priority list for people to aspire towards, is extremely important for India. We are a poor country. Poor countries can't do much for their citizens; it's as simple as that. So we either keep ourselves poor and scramble for whatever little we have, or we grow the pie.

Becoming a rich country has other advantages. People have a higher standard of living. Corruption generally declines in rich countries. Education and healthcare quality improves. More liberal thought processes set in. At least in rich democracies, issues like communalism and racism decline.

Therefore, should we not set aside our other differences and make all efforts to make India rich for the next thirty years? Note that 10 per cent growth for thirty years will make the average income rise seventeen times. If we grow at 5 per cent or so, it will rise just four times. There is a huge difference in what India can become, in our lifetime, if we manage our economy properly.

So how does one grow at 10 per cent? Well, these are the ingredients. First, a stable and action-oriented government. Second, a pro-business economic mindset with reduced government controls in most sectors. Third, an intangible but highly critical element called investor confidence, which means investors are willing to put their money in India and hope to make a return from it.

Restoring India to its growth path is the single biggest issue. This is not to say that other issues are not important. However, without a strong economy, none of the other good stuff happens. A rich, prosperous India should be every Indian's dream. Only then will we be able to give the youth their due.

Scored Low in Exams? Some Life Lessons from a 76-Percenter

> Over time in life, the marks will stop.
> What will matter is what people think of you.

As a 90 per cent aggregate in class X and XII becomes as common as kissing in our movies (no big deal) and cut-offs for good colleges become insane, we wonder if there is anyone who hasn't scored amazing marks. In the noise of high scorers, we often forget the lakhs of students who score in the fifties, sixties and seventies. We brand them mediocre. We offer them succour with a few articles that cite low scorers who became billionaires or movie stars and have headlines that scream 'Marks Don't Matter'. Well, if they didn't matter, why on earth would everyone be chasing them, is a question they don't answer.

This article is addressed to those low scorers. It's for that average guy X who scored, say, a 76 per cent in his boards. X, the overweight kid who isn't that confident and has become even less so after the results came out. X, whose relatives and neighbours come to console him with 'it doesn't matter', but deep down wonder if this boy will do anything in life. If you relate to this guy, or know someone who does, this chapter is for you. It isn't a soothing balm for your low marks. These are some no-nonsense tips on what to do when you have scores that suck and people have given up on you. Here goes:

1. You are not your marks

Yes, marks are important. They make life much, much easier. High marks make people think you are smart. Colleges with a brand name let you come in. Companies with a brand name come to these colleges. They give you a job, which pays rather well. You can use that money to pay bills, get married, have sex, start a family and produce kids whom you will push to get higher marks and repeat the cycle of torment. This, for most people, is life—making it as predictable, safe and stable as possible.

Indian parents particularly love this zero-risk-appetite life, where a monthly cash flow is assured and kids are born and raised as per plan. They have a word for it—settled. Indians love that word. We want to settle, we don't want to roam, have adventures and fly. Settle, or in other words, produce kids, work in office, watch TV at home, repeat for a few decades, die. Toppers find it easier to settle. Non-toppers take a bit longer. A delay in 'settling', the ultimate Indian dream, is just about the only sucky thing about low marks.

2. The game of life is not over

These marks are in certain subjects, which are not exactly what lead to success in life. Sure, you study maths and science, but these are standard concepts, recycled and drilled into students and tested in the exams. The only thing high marks indicate is that the student has the tenacity and perseverance to excel at something. Hence, I am not going to say toppers don't deserve praise. But life is more than just tenacity and mathematics. Exams don't test creativity, imagination, people skills and communication. In life, these are what matter. You build these skills through study or actual practice, and it is highly likely you will get somewhere in life. However, you must add hard work to it. Ask yourself whether you got low marks because of lack of aptitude or because of laziness. If you slacked off, don't do that again if you want to get anywhere in life. Take that lesson, and then build your communication, English and people skills. Learn how business works. Not everyone in India can get a plum job, there are just way too many of us. Entrepreneurship is something a lot of youngsters will have to learn and try.

3. Strive for excellence

In whatever you do, try to excel. Excellence in board exams can be measured through marks, but over time in life, the marks will stop. What will matter is what people think of you. Your reputation, your reliability and your word will build your own mini-brand. Once that happens, people will stop asking about your marks, or where you studied. You will be the brand.

Nobody has asked me for my marks in a long time. However, you know the boy I wrote about earlier? Well, that's me. I scored that 76 per cent in class X. I felt horrible then, but eventually I didn't let it define me. It doesn't matter today. After all, you still read this article, right?

Concluding Thoughts

I'm delighted you've read my book. I hope the various issues raised in it resonated with you at some level. The road to awesomeness is long and difficult for India. The journey may be tough, but it is not impossible. If we fix our governance, societal values, equality and resources, we will get there.

There will be noise, dirty politics, naysayers, indifference and aligned biases all around us. The challenge will be for us to keep our dream alive despite all these hurdles. To be singularly focused on what will make India a better place, and base our opinion on any issue only on that criterion. There will be no villains and messiahs, and there won't be any place for mindless fandom or hatred. To fix India, we need to be practical, rational and scientific. It doesn't mean we lose our humanity and compassion, but that we don't let emotions sway decisions taken in the national interest.

One of the questions I get asked a lot is: what can I do as an ordinary individual, with no authority, power or influential voice? Well, here are some pointers on what you can do to make India awesome:

1. **Excel in your field**: Whatever you do, try to be the best at it. There is too much mediocrity all around and we have learnt to live with it. However, awesomeness has no place for mediocrity. And do not confuse excellence with elitism. Being excellent at your work is different from considering yourself superior to others.

2. **Realize it is not just the government's job (or that of politicians) to make India better**: If you look back in history, the people who have made India awesome aren't all politicians. Most of the people that did this are not from the government. Whether it is entrepreneurs like J.R.D. Tata and N.R. Narayana Murthy, sportspersons like Sachin Tendulkar or musicians like A.R. Rahman, people from all walks of life have helped improve our nation. Not just celebrities, but E. Sreedharan, responsible for the Delhi Metro, and Dr Verghese Kurien, who created the Amul revolution, were all ordinary people doing their work extraordinarily well. Mahatma Gandhi and Swami Vivekananda, two of the most influential figures in India's history, never held political office. Aim to be one of those people who made India awesome.

3. **Back the issue, not the person**: It is too easy to latch on to a messiah and worship him as your hero. But it's irresponsible to do that with a politician. Politicians make decisions and, like with all humans, not every decision they make is right. You should be able to be critical when your favourite politician does wrong, even if it means getting out of your cosy club of supporters. Similarly, you should be able to praise when the politician you don't like does something good. You are here to back India, not an individual.

4. **Be modern, scientific and open-minded**: The world is changing. Unless you are at the cutting edge of technology and modern thought, you will be left behind. Preserve tradition, history, culture and religion; at the same time be willing to change for the better. Chest-thumping about one's past is usually a sign of inadequacy about the present. Drop regressive values in the name of Indian culture. The new Indian culture is to continuously evolve, change and adapt until we reach awesome levels.

5. **Use your social network with the best possible intention**: Everyone doesn't reach millions of people. However, most of you do have a reach of hundreds through your social media accounts. Why not post your views about the nation there? If everyone devoted 10 per cent of their status updates to issues relating to the country, we would have a far more vibrant societal debate and dialogue in this country. Post those party selfies, but also type in a few lines about what you feel about a particular issue. Did any article in this book touch you or make you think? Why not share it and get other people's views on your social accounts?

6. **Cut the negativity**: Any discussion on national issues quickly descends into slanging matches, outrage, anger, hatred and abuse. This is negativity we can do without. Whether among friends, family or in a nation, conflicts and differences of opinion will exist. Why not discuss issues in a civil manner and work them out creatively? Have you ever had a great solution come to you when you were angry? We need to be calm. Else, we achieve nothing.

I hope you enjoyed this book and feel inspired to create solutions for India yourself. Once again, I thank you and even salute you for reading a book on national issues. People like you are my hope for this nation. Let us join hands, and together let us take this great nation to where it truly deserves to be. Let us work now so our grandkids can say one day, 'I'll tell you something about my grandparents' generation. They were just awesome!'